Healing After the Trauma Bond

Women Who Break Bonds and Emerge Stronger

Jennifer Alushan

© **Copyright 2023 - All rights reserved.**

The content contained within this book may not be reproduced, duplicated or transmitted without direct written permission from the author or the publisher.

Under no circumstances will any blame or legal responsibility be held against the publisher, or author, for any damages, reparation, or monetary loss due to the information contained within this book, either directly or indirectly.

Legal Notice:

This book is copyright protected. It is only for personal use. You cannot amend, distribute, sell, use, quote or paraphrase any part, or the content within this book, without the consent of the author or publisher.

Disclaimer Notice:

Please note the information contained within this document is for educational and entertainment purposes only. All effort has been executed to present accurate, up to date, reliable, complete information. No warranties of any kind are declared or implied. Readers acknowledge that the author is not engaged in the rendering of legal, financial, medical or professional advice. The content within this book has been derived from various sources. Please consult a licensed professional before attempting any techniques outlined in this book.

By reading this document, the reader agrees that under no circumstances is the author responsible for any losses, direct or indirect, that are incurred as a result of the use of the information contained within this document, including, but not limited to, errors, omissions, or inaccuracies.

Table of Contents

INTRODUCTION 1

CHAPTER 1: HOPE AND RECOVERY—BREAKING TRAUMA 5
BONDS AND RECLAIMING SPACE 5
    ACKNOWLEDGMENT 6
    TAKING A STEP BACK 7
    THE LIGHT AT THE END OF THE TUNNEL 9
    YOU ARE RESILIENT 10
    CREATING A SPACE FOR HEALING 12

CHAPTER 2: TRAUMA BONDS—UNPACKING DYSFUNCTIONAL TRAITS IN
RELATIONSHIPS... 15
    WHAT IS A TRAUMA BOND? 15
    TRAITS OF A DYSFUNCTIONAL RELATIONSHIP 17
    SEVEN STAGES OF TRAUMA BONDING 20
        1.   *Love Bombing* 20
        2.   *Trust and Dependency* 21
        3.   *Criticism and Devaluation* 21
        4.   *Manipulation and Gaslighting* 22
        5.   *Resignation and Submission* 22
        6.   *Disconnection to a Sense of Self* 23
        7.   *Emotional Addiction* 23
    TRAITS OF A HEALTHY RELATIONSHIP 24

CHAPTER 3: THE CYCLE OF ABUSE—RESPONSIVE BEHAVIORS THAT PERPETUATE
IT 29
    THE CYCLE OF ABUSE 30
        1.   *Tension Buildup* 30
        2.   *Abuse Incidence* 31
        3.   *Reconciliation* 31
        4.   *Calm Before the Storm* 32
        5.   *Discard Phase* 33
        6.   *Hoovering Phase* 33
    HOW IT PERSISTS 34

COPING MECHANISMS THAT KEEP US STUCK 37

CHAPTER 4: RECLAIMING SAFETY—HEALING AFTER ABUSE 43

IMPORTANCE OF BOUNDARIES FOR HEALING AFTER TRAUMA 43
   Boundary Setting Basics 46
BOUNDARIES WITH YOUR ABUSIVE EX 47
   Physical Boundaries 48
   Emotional Boundaries 48
   Other Boundaries Concerning Safety 49
BOUNDARIES WHEN YOU NEED TO CO-PARENT WITH AN ABUSER 49
BOUNDARIES WITH FAMILY AND FRIENDS 52
FINANCIAL BOUNDARIES 54
PERSONAL BOUNDARIES 56
BEING ALONE 57

CHAPTER 5: FINANCIAL RECOVERY—REBUILDING SECURITY AND FREEDOM 61

FINANCIAL ABUSE AND STRESS 62
ASSESS YOUR FINANCES—FOCUS ON THE DATA 63
   1. Know Your Credit Score 64
   2. Create a Comprehensive Budget 64
      a. 50/30/20 budget: 64
      b. The 80/20 budget 65
      c. Envelope method: 65
   3. Calculate Your Debt-To-Income Ratio 66
TAKE ACTION—SOONER THAN LATER 66
   1. Open a Bank Account and Begin Saving 67
   2. Create a Strategy for Dealing With Credit Card Debt 67
   3. Improve Your Credit Score 68

CHAPTER 6: EMBRACING JOY—DISCOVERING YOUR LIGHT AND COMMITTING TO POSITIVE CHANGE 71

TAKE CARE OF YOUR BODY AND MIND 72
LET NATURE IN 73
CONNECT WITH ANIMALS 74
TAKE PLEASURE IN ROUTINE ACTIVITIES 75
STEP OUTSIDE 77
TACKLE A PROJECT 78
ART 79
FITNESS 80
SPIRITUAL 82
   Exercise 84
      Creating a Pleasure and Gratitude Calendar 84
      Nurturing Support 85
      Gratitude Reflection 85

CHAPTER 7: NAVIGATING SETBACKS—BUILDING A 87

FOUNDATION OF SELF-LOVE AND RESILIENCE 87
- COMMON SETBACKS...88
- HOW TO PLAN FOR SETBACKS AND DEAL WITH THEM.........................91
  - *Exercise*...93
    - Overwhelming Sadness 93
    - Frustration 94
    - Overwhelming Anger or Rage...94

CHAPTER 8: REWRITING YOUR NARRATIVE—DEFINING 97

YOUR OWN PATH 97
- YOUR VALUES, DREAMS, AND GOALS 98
  - *Your Character*..99
  - *Emotional* 100
  - *Intellectual*..101
  - *Life's Purpose*..102
  - *Family*...103
  - *Social* 104
  - *Health and Fitness*..105
  - *Finances*..106
  - *Career*...107
  - *Personal Space* 108
  - *Spirituality* 109
- SETTING THE GROUNDWORK TO SUPPORT YOUR GROWTH 110
  - *Connect to Your Inner Child*...112
  - *Own Your Power*...113
  - *Your Vision*..115
  - *Your Goal Statement* 117
  - *Exercise: The Tree of Life Concept* 118

CHAPTER 9: FROM DREAMS TO ACTION—STRATEGIZING............121

YOUR WAY TO FULFILLMENT...121
- SHORT-TERM AND LONG-TERM GOALS 122
- TAKING ACTION 123
  - *Create an Action Plan* 123
  - *Identify Obstacles* 125
  - *Track Your Progress*..126
  - *Schedule Reviews and Re-evaluations*.............................126
  - *Celebrate Your Wins* 127
- SEEING IT THROUGH 128
  - *Remember Your Why*..128

Visualize Success..*129*
Create an Environment for Success *130*
Utilize Constructive Outlets for Your Emotions..........................*131*
Prioritize Your Actions Over Their Results *132*
Practice Tenacity *132*
Work With a Coach *133*
Exercise: The 1-3-5 Rule..*133*

CHAPTER 10: REDEFINING YOURSELF—CELEBRATING GROWTH AND PROGRESS 135

Reflect on How Your Life Has Changed..136
Embrace Your Changes 136
Self-Love 137
Self-Care 138
Celebrate Your Growth..139
Look to the Future 140

CONCLUSION 143

REFERENCES...147

Introduction

If you're reading this, I imagine you've had the courage to leave a toxic relationship, but the wounds it inflicted remain. You find yourself entangled in the aftermath of a trauma bond, dealing with emotions ranging from confusion to fear to heartbreak. As a fellow survivor, I want you to know you are not alone. I've been there, and I know it's not an easy road. That's why I wrote this book; as a compassionate friend who understands. Together, we'll look at how to heal after ending a traumatic relationship.

Trauma bonds are pervasive and crippling, trapping people in emotionally and psychologically damaging relationships. They can take many forms, ranging from toxic romantic relationships to abusive family dynamics. The emotional connection formed in trauma bonds is intense and profound, making escape seem impossible.

If you are trapped in a trauma bond, know that you are not alone. It's a difficult journey to break free from these bonds, but it's not impossible. In this book, we'll look at the various types of trauma bonds, how they affect people, and how you can break free and reclaim your power.

It takes more than just leaving a toxic relationship to break free from trauma bonds. It entails identifying the underlying patterns and behaviors that keep you stuck, as well as learning how to recognize and avoid them in the future. By doing this, you can overcome the trauma and come out of it stronger and more resilient than ever.

In the following chapters, we'll look at different aspects of trauma bonds and offer actionable steps toward healing and growth. You will learn how to identify and address the underlying causes of trauma bonds, as well as how to set healthy boundaries and rediscover your self-worth.

Any form of abuse alters the chemicals in our brains that regulate emotions, anxiety, and depression, resulting in complex and post-traumatic stress disorders that can be debilitating. This book is not intended to minimize the horrific effects of trauma, nor is it a substitute for trauma-focused therapy or medical interventions. Its purpose is to validate that your trauma and abuse were real and that they were not your fault.

Recognizing trauma, dysfunction, and pain is the first step toward healing. It takes enormous courage to confront the impact of emotional abuse, narcissism, and post-traumatic relationship syndrome (PTRS). This guide will provide a compassionate and hopeful perspective on the path to taking your power back and finding peace and joy.

I am an ardent advocate for leading a healthy lifestyle, fostering healthy relationships, and empowering women because I have personally seen the effects of trauma and dysfunction in my own life and as an educator. I've worked with students and families who have experienced trauma. Despite growing up in a family that appeared functional on the outside, the dysfunction beneath the surface catalyzed a series of poor relationship choices and painful mistakes in my life. These events, however, set me on a path of healing, growth, and rebuilding. With over 30 years of experience as an educator and a B.S. and Master's degree in the field, I am committed to assisting others on their own healing journey.

In the pages that follow, we will look at the behavioral patterns of emotional abusers and how their actions are based on their own deficits and unmet needs. While you have no influence over their decisions, you do have influence over your own healing journey. You have the potential to become unstoppable once you are able to break free from the trauma bond and invite nurturing, healing, and self-love into your life. Your time alone can provide you with strength, wisdom, healing, and peace as you continue on your path to health and joy.

This journey will inspire you to look within for answers to your liberation. Giving the abuser unlimited mental energy only diminishes your own power and keeps you trapped in a victim mentality. It's time to work through your pain and fears and reach your full potential. It's possible to find peace and joy on the other side of trauma, and this book is here to give you hope and support as you move through the healing process.

This book is intended for women who have experienced dysfunctional relationships and trauma as children, adolescents, or even in their adult lives. It acknowledges that, while you cannot change the fact that you have experienced trauma, you can work to lessen its impact over time. It emphasizes the importance of replacing toxic interactions with healthy ones and listening to your intuition in order to build a happy life. It acknowledges that feeling vulnerable and uncertain about the future is normal, but it also emphasizes your inner strength to create stability and peace.

Remember that you are not alone on your journey to discovering yourself and regaining your power. Many others have gone down this road before you and found healing and growth on the other side of their trauma. You have everything you need to break free from trauma bonds and create a brighter future for yourself with just a little guidance from the strategies, insights, and support provided in this book.

You have the ability to heal, set healthy boundaries, and rediscover your self-worth. You deserve healthy relationships, peace, and happiness. You possess the ability to overcome the effects of trauma and live a life free of the shackles of past trauma. Be patient with yourself and take the necessary steps toward healing and empowerment. You are more powerful than you realize, and you have the ability to design a life filled with happiness, fulfillment, and well-being.

Remember that healing is a process that takes time. However, with patience, self-compassion, and the strategies outlined in this book, you can break free from trauma bonds and emerge stronger, healthier, and more empowered.

May this book be a guide and a source of hope for you as you continue on your path to healing and reclaiming your power. You have the ability to break free from trauma bonds and live a life filled with love, joy, and empowerment. It's time to put your health first and work toward a happier, healthier future.

Chapter 1:

Hope and Recovery—Breaking Trauma Bonds and Reclaiming Space

When we become entangled in the web of a traumatic bond, it can feel suffocating, overwhelming, and seemingly impossible to break free. The emotional bonds that bind us to the abuser can be powerful, making it difficult to assert our own needs and prioritize our healing. However, there is always hope. In this chapter, we'll look at the process of breaking trauma bonds and reclaiming space for our own healing. We will explore the empowering process of discovering our own resiliency and separating ourselves from the abuse and trauma bonds in order to make room for our own healing and growth.

This chapter is a helping hand for those who have felt the grip of trauma bonds, as well as a guide for navigating the path to healing, self-empowerment, and reclaiming our own space. Let's begin this transformative journey together.

Acknowledgment

Leaving an abusive relationship is a harrowing experience that can leave long-lasting emotional scars. Many survivors attempt to minimize the severity of their trauma in order to shield themselves from the painful and overwhelming emotions that accompany it. It's normal to feel ashamed or embarrassed about what happened, and some people may even try to bury those memories in the hopes of forgetting them. However, it's critical to recognize that what you went through was real and valid, and that it's okay to experience the full range of emotions that come with it. You are not alone, and your experiences count.

It's essential to recognize that denying the reality of abuse only delays the healing process and prevents survivors from engaging in the necessary work to detoxify trauma. Many survivors tend to compare their experiences with others, believing that another person's trauma is greater than their own, making it difficult for them to acknowledge their pain and suffering. When survivors' trauma is minimized, they are robbed of the self-compassion they need to heal and move forward. It's imperative that you make an effort to validate your own feelings and experiences, even if they differ from those of others.

To show compassion towards oneself, one must first confront one's own pain, hurt, and suffering. Recognizing and accepting these difficult emotions is the first step toward healing and recovery. We can only begin to alleviate distress and pain by facing it. By practicing self-compassion, we can validate our wounds and cultivate a deeper sense of gentleness and kindness toward ourselves. This self-compassion gives survivors the strength and resilience to persevere through the difficult journey of post-trauma growth and eventually thrive.

When you decide to acknowledge and confront the abuse you endured, keep in mind that you may experience the same emotions you did at the time the abuse resurfaced. It's natural to feel the pain, hurt, and suffering that have been building up inside of you. However, only by accepting and working through these emotions can you begin to heal.

You must be willing to admit the extent of your injuries and seek the appropriate help to heal. This process of accepting the reality of the abuse can be painful and uncomfortable, but it's a necessary step in moving forward.

Abusers frequently trick their victims into believing they are to blame for the abuse. However, it's critical to remember that true narcissistic behavior is unlikely to change and that you did not cause the abuse. Recognize that the only person responsible for the abuse is the abuser themselves. Acknowledging this truth allows you to reclaim control of your life and approach the situation with clarity. It's not your fault, and you are not deserving of it. It's time to take control of your life and move on.

For the long-term well-being of abuse survivors, it is crucial to acknowledge and treat the emotional suffering they have experienced. The notion that some types of suffering are more severe than others can be harmful, preventing survivors from receiving the care and support they require (Dillmann, 2011). Regardless of how abuse compares to other forms of suffering, it's crucial to reject this idea and instead focus on accepting and recovering from the pain it has caused. Survivors have a right to compassion, gentleness, healing, and growth, and seeking professional help can be a helpful step in that process.

To begin the healing process, survivors must resist the urge to minimize their experiences, acknowledge the reality of the abuse, and seek help. You must approach this process with self-compassion, accept painful emotions, and let go of beliefs that are impeding your healing and ultimate well-being. All of these are important steps toward becoming a thriving post-trauma individual.

Taking a Step Back

In the aftermath of an abusive relationship, it can be difficult to make sense of the trauma and damage caused. Allowing yourself emotional and physical space to process the pain and grieve is essential. It's important to remember that emotional pain, like physical pain, can have a serious impact on our bodies. Recovery takes time and requires assistance. Therapy, as well as a strong support system, can be an important part of the healing process. You don't have to go through the healing process by yourself. Remember to be gentle with yourself and give yourself the time and space you need to heal.

Recognizing the impact of abuse on the healing process is critical. Abuse can take many forms, including physical, emotional, and sexual abuse, and it can be perpetrated by family members, friends, romantic partners, or coworkers. Regardless of the type, all forms of abuse can have negative long-term and short-term consequences. Even minor abuse can cause physical and mental distress, such as confusion, shame, fear, mood swings, and muscle tension. It's critical to recognize these consequences and understand that they are not the victim's fault. The first step in healing is acknowledging the reality of abuse and seeking assistance in getting better.

When abuse continues for an extended period of time, the victim's mental and emotional well-being can suffer greatly. Long-term abuse can cause anxiety and depression, feelings of guilt and shame, sleep disturbances, social isolation, and a weakened sense of self-worth. Chronic pain, eating disorders, substance abuse issues, and even suicidal thoughts or actions may develop in the victim. To cope with the trauma of abuse, it's critical to recognize the severity of these symptoms and seek support and care.

It can be beneficial to pause and take a step back from our lives from time to time, especially after a traumatic event. During this difficult time, strengthening our bonds with loved ones and our community can be a huge source of support and comfort. We can regain control of our lives by reassessing our personal goals and devising a plan to achieve them. Giving back through volunteering or charitable acts can provide a sense of purpose and fulfillment, assisting us in overcoming stress and trauma. Remember that it's important to take care of ourselves during difficult times, and reaching out for help and finding healthy ways to cope can make all the difference.

Learning about abuse can be a crucial step toward healing and progress. By educating yourself about the signs of abuse and why it occurs, you can gain valuable insights and distance yourself from the situation.

Understanding the dynamics of abusive relationships can also help you be more compassionate and kind to yourself, as you realize you're not alone and the abuse isn't your fault. So, read about abuse, educate yourself, and be gentle with yourself as you begin the healing process. This can also be an overwhelming process, so make sure to take breaks as and when you need them.

If you are struggling to recover from the trauma of abuse, seeking the assistance of a therapist can be a great first step toward regaining control of your life. Going through the motions on your own can be exhausting, confusing, and overwhelming. A therapist can provide support and direction by assisting you in processing your emotions, identifying negative thought patterns, and developing coping skills to help you move forward. Journaling is another useful tool for processing emotions and reflecting on your progress over time. It can provide a safe space for you to express your thoughts and feelings while also assisting you in gaining a better understanding of your experiences. Remember that healing takes time and self-compassion, and there is no shame in seeking help to begin the road to recovery.

It can be emotionally draining and traumatizing to leave an abusive relationship. It's critical to recognize the reality of the situation and understand the impact of abuse. Survivors can heal and move forward by taking a step back, educating themselves, seeking help, and practicing self-compassion. It may not be an easy journey, but it's one that must be undertaken in order to reclaim control of one's life and chart a course toward a healthier, happier future. Remember that healing takes time, but it's possible to thrive after trauma with the right tools and support.

The Light at the End of the Tunnel

Breaking a trauma bond and breaking the cycle of abuse takes tremendous courage. It's not easy, and the suffering is palpable, both emotionally and physically. But there is hope and happiness waiting for you on the other side.

It's critical to remove yourself from the toxic relationship in order to process what happened and avoid returning to it. You've probably left and returned several times, but the abuse continues because you keep returning. It helps to be patient and compassionate with yourself as you heal. Remind yourself that it's normal to be confused, scared, tense, angry, or any other emotion that arises. These emotions are a normal part of the healing process, and there is no need to rush through them. They are yours, and it's okay to sit with and experience them. Sitting through and experiencing painful feelings makes you nothing but brave.

There is no definitive answer to how long it takes to recover from any type of abusive relationship. But developing a safety plan, prioritizing self-care, and self-love, working with a therapist, setting boundaries, connecting with support groups, and seeking out other resources can help alleviate the pain. It's important to understand that you are not alone. Being a survivor restores your identity, but you will remain a victim as long as you deny that about yourself (Survivor Stories, 2019).

Even after a traumatic event, it's important to remember that it's okay to feel joy, celebrate successes, and bask in the warmth of family and friends. It's all part of the process of healing. This may be a long and arduous journey, but there is a light at the end of the tunnel, and you have the strength to find it. Never give up hope and keep moving forward. You will emerge stronger and wiser on the other side.

You Are Resilient

Even after you leave an abusive relationship, you may feel weak, powerless, and trapped. However, it's critical to remember that you are strong and resilient and that you have been through difficult times before. You may have realized that you wanted more than just to survive and sought assistance to learn how to take better care of yourself. Although the aftermath of traumatic experiences can be difficult, safety and reassurance are critical for long-term well-being.

Remember that you are not alone in this. The right people, people with good energy, will understand and support you. Building and maintaining such healthy connections can aid in healing.

Following this experience, you might lose faith in your sense of judgment, intuition, or self. But at this point, it's crucial to maintain your resilience. Recognize the forces that were against you and the circumstances that were beyond your control. Recognize the strength it took to walk away and choose your own survival and well-being.

When you show up for yourself, it can help you build trust and discover your inner strength. Although you can't change what happened in the past, you can change how you react to and interpret it. One way to do this is by looking towards the future and its new possibilities and noticing any subtle ways in which you may already feel better as you deal with challenging situations.

Going through a traumatic experience can be extremely overwhelming, and it's critical to recognize that healing is a process. As you progress, you may come across opportunities for self-discovery and growth. Many trauma survivors report improved relationships, a stronger sense of self-worth, a stronger spiritual connection, and a greater appreciation for life (American Trauma Society, 2017). It's critical to cultivate your sense of self-worth and confidence in your ability to overcome obstacles. Taking care of yourself through activities you enjoy, self-care, and regular exercise can help you stay strong and ready to face any situation that comes your way. Remember that your healing journey is unique, and it's okay to take it one step at a time.

Remember that many women leave for the final time and never return. They finally realize that if they keep returning to their situation, nothing will change. They rewrite their own stories to make them look the way they want them to. Remember that you are strong and capable of choosing your own path. The road may not be easy, but you can boost your resilience by staying connected, cultivating a positive self-image, and taking care of yourself. Believe in yourself, and keep in mind that you are not alone.

Creating a Space for Healing

When it comes to healing after abuse, giving yourself space to recover is critical. You must prioritize your emotional and physical well-being and establish a safe environment for yourself. Instead of concentrating on your abuser, turn your attention to your own needs. It's critical to remember that you did not cause the abuse and that there was nothing you could have done to prevent it. Abuse is all about power and control, so the abuse would have continued even if you had acted differently. You should be proud of yourself for having the courage and determination to make a positive change in your life. You are deserving of a life free of abuse and filled with joy.

When someone has endured abuse, it can leave deep emotional scars that are difficult to heal. It can also make trusting others difficult, leaving you feeling isolated and disconnected from healthy relationships. Social isolation can make it even more difficult to overcome the aftereffects of abuse by keeping you down and dependent on unhealthy relationships.

But there is still hope. Reconnecting with others can help you feel less alone and provide the support you need to start the healing process. While it can be difficult to trust others after being abused, it's necessary to take that leap and allow others to support you. You do not have to go through this by yourself.

While you are under no obligation to do anything you do not wish to do, finding a trusted friend or family member who will listen to you without judgment and offer empathy and compassion can be a great source of comfort and healing. If you don't have anyone to turn to in your personal life, consider joining a support group for abuse survivors. You can find a safe space to share your feelings and work through your emotions by connecting with others who have gone through similar experiences.

Stay patient and compassionate with yourself as you go through the healing process. It's normal to feel confused, scared, tense, or angry, and these feelings are part of the healing process. There's no need to rush through them, and it's important to sit with them and experience them. Remember that you are deserving of love and respect. Healing takes time and support, but you can reclaim your life and find peace.

Chapter 2:

Trauma Bonds—Unpacking Dysfunctional Traits in Relationships

Trauma can be a crippling and destructive force in a person's life, often resulting in long-term psychological and emotional damage. While the effects of trauma vary greatly from person to person, it's clear that dysfunctional behaviors and responses can play a significant role in the long-term perpetuation of this harm. In this chapter, we'll look at how dysfunctional behaviors can interact and evolve to form a cycle of trauma that can be difficult to break. Understanding the dynamics at work in these situations allows us to start developing strategies for breaking free from the cycle and leading a healthier, more fulfilling life.

What Is a Trauma Bond?

Trauma bonding is a complex and emotional attachment that forms in a relationship where there is a cyclical pattern of abuse between an abused person and their abuser. In this pattern, the abuser typically follows up abusive behavior with acts of kindness and affection toward the victim, which results in a never-ending cycle. This cycle of abuse and positive reinforcement forms an impenetrable bond.

Abuse of any kind, including emotional, physical, or sexual abuse, can result in the trauma that leads to this bond. The effects of this trauma can be long-lasting and have serious psychological and physical consequences. A trauma bond can form after weeks, months, or even years of abuse, but not everyone who is abused forms one.

Trauma bonding can make leaving an abusive situation difficult because the abused person may feel attached to and dependent on the abuser. This attachment can be perplexing and overwhelming because it involves positive and loving feelings toward the abuser. The abuser wields enormous power and control, which, when combined with shame and embarrassment, makes it nearly impossible for the abused partner to leave.

Relationship trauma has been recognized after researchers studied people who had been abused and discovered symptoms similar to those seen in PTSD (Dexter, 2022). However, relationship trauma affects a person's ability to avoid triggers or stimuli associated with the trauma in a different way than PTSD does. Because the cycle of abuse and positive reinforcement makes it nearly impossible to avoid triggers, it is very challenging for victims to break free from the cycle of abuse.

Domestic abuse is not the only source of trauma bonds. They can also occur as a result of child abuse, incestuous relationships, elder abuse, exploitative employment, abduction or hostage situations, human trafficking, and high-control religious settings. In all of these cases, the abused person becomes reliant on their abuser for a sense of safety and security, making it extremely difficult to break the cycle of abuse.

Trauma bonding is more than just a difficult relationship; it's rooted in our fundamental need for connection and security. The abused person develops feelings of sympathy and loyalty toward their abuser, making it difficult for them to leave the situation. Abuse and love are inextricably linked, making it difficult for the victim of abuse to distinguish between the two.

Understanding the dynamics of trauma bonding is critical for recognizing, processing, and healing the emotional wounds that have resulted from it. Leaving an abusive relationship can be a complicated and difficult process that necessitates empathy, understanding, and support. Understanding the dynamics at work in these situations allows us to start developing strategies for breaking free from the cycle and leading a healthier, more fulfilling life.

Traits of a Dysfunctional Relationship

Toxic relationships may manifest in a variety of ways, and the signs of toxicity can be subtle or unmistakable, depending on the nature of the relationship. Although identifying red flags in the midst of a toxic relationship can be complicated, it's critical to be aware of any signs that could indicate unhealthy behavior and take steps to address the issue right away.

You may come to understand that as the relationship developed, you began to exhibit similar toxic behaviors in order to survive:

- **Patterns of disrespect:** Chronic tardiness, failure to honor commitments, and other behaviors that show a disregard for your time may indicate abusive behavior. While some people struggle with punctuality, it's important to consider the frequency and context of these actions.

- **Stonewalling:** This is the act of withdrawing from a conversation or interaction and refusing to engage or communicate. Giving one-word answers, changing the subject, or completely ignoring the other person are all examples of this.

- **Manipulation:** This is a common tactic used to control and exploit the victim. It entails employing techniques such as guilt-tripping, gaslighting, and lying in order to maintain power over the victim and perpetuate the cycle of abuse:

    o **Gaslighting:** Gaslighting is a deceptive and abusive technique used to instill self-doubt in the victim, causing them to doubt their emotions, intuition, and sanity. The abuser denies events, even when the victim recalls them vividly and frequently blames the victim for the relationship's problems.

  - **Dishonesty:** This means employing deceptive tactics to influence or control another person in order to achieve the abuser's own goals. This type of behavior is harmful because it undermines the victim's trust and autonomy, frequently resulting in emotional and psychological harm.

  - **Guilt-tripping:** This is when the abuser attempts to hold the victim accountable for their own negative actions or emotions. The abuser instills guilt, shame, and a false sense of responsibility for things beyond the victim's control by manipulating their emotions.

- **Lack of empathy:** This allows abusers to disregard the feelings and experiences of their victims, contributing to emotional and psychological abuse. This behavior is especially present in those with narcissistic personality disorder.

- **Extreme anger:** This is a common trait in abusers, and it frequently leads to physical or emotional abuse of their victims. Anger out of control can have serious consequences and lead to destructive behavior.

- **Extreme envy or jealousy:** Abusers who exhibit extreme envy and jealousy may manipulate and control their partner, resulting in disastrous consequences. This can result in constant suspicion and mistrust in the relationship and escalate to the point of accusing the victim of infidelity and isolation from loved ones, with the abuser frequently behaving rudely towards them.

- **Belittling:** Abusers put down and make fun of their victims' intelligence, appearance, and mental health. They make negative comparisons to others and say things like, "No one else can put up with you."

- **Threats:** Abusers may resort to yelling, sulking, or intentionally damaging your belongings. They may also threaten violence against you, your loved ones, or even pets as a means of control.

- **Physical and sexual violence:** The abuser may push, shove, hit, or grab the victim. They may coerce or manipulate the victim into performing unwanted sexual acts or behaviors. They could also cause harm to the victim's pets or family members.

- **Controlling and possessive behaviors:** The abuser keeps tabs on the victim's movements, engagements, and companions. They seek to exert control over their social circle and become enraged when their commands are disregarded.

- **Financial restrictions:** Abusers demonstrate poor financial behavior by controlling income, restricting access to personal accounts and credit cards, and providing a daily allowance, forcing victims to seek permission for additional funds.

- **Passive aggressive behavior:** This involves using indirect and subtle methods to express anger, hostility, or resentment, such as silent treatment, sarcastic remarks, or intentionally forgetting to do something.

- **Threatening self-harm:** The abuser uses the threat of hurting or killing themselves to control their victim. It can make the victim feel guilty and responsible for the actions of the abuser. It's critical to understand that assisting the abuser does not imply agreeing to their demands or remaining in a dangerous situation.

- **Lack of accountability:** This refers to the abuser's refusal to accept responsibility for their harmful behavior. They may blame the victim, deny, or minimize their actions, and refuse to make amends or change their behavior.

- **Isolation:** Abusive partners use emotional manipulation to isolate their victims from their support network. They may take your phone, answer it, and say you're busy, or they may cause your plans to be canceled. They may even persuade you that your loved ones don't want to hear from you or that they don't understand your relationship.

Seven Stages of Trauma Bonding

The seven stages of trauma bonding often start as positive relationships before becoming abusive (Laub, 2023). This progression can have a profound impact on a victim's worldview, perception of reality, and relationship with themselves.

1. Love Bombing

Love bombing occurs when an abuser uses excessive flattery and high praise to create a strong sense of "connection" in the relationship. This encompasses using the phrase "I love you" in a suspiciously premature manner within the relationship, as well as employing exaggerated demonstrations of attention, charm, and affection with the intention of manipulating you.

By preying on the victim's emotional needs and causing them to let down their guard, this can set the stage for an abusive dynamic in a trauma bond. It can elicit positive emotions, validate the victim, demonstrate the abuser's intentions, and provide a sense of stability and security. Though the abuser may appear oblivious to their manipulation at times, this is rarely the case in a trauma bond.

2. Trust and Dependency

An abuser will work hard at first to gain their victim's trust by making commitments and suggesting moving in together or getting married. However, once they have gained your trust, they will withdraw from the commitment. They begin to distance themselves and test your trust as you grow attached, making you feel guilty for questioning them. The dependency, which was already well established during the stage of the love bombing, is exacerbated by this.

It's normal to feel doubtful in a healthy relationship, and it's critical to take the time necessary to truly understand someone, not just through their words but also through their actions. While trauma bonding creates an illusion of trust and affection, a healthy relationship always embodies love, acceptance, and validation without ever leaving you craving for them (Being, 2022).

3. Criticism and Devaluation

When abusers gain your trust, they will begin to scrutinize various aspects of your personality and label them as insignificant or problematic. The criticism can sometimes feel abrupt, especially after experiencing a love bombing, but abusers will typically wait until they have fully established trust before beginning to criticize their victim. The transition to this phase of criticism can be subtle, and you may misinterpret it as a natural progression in the relationship.

Emotional abusers become increasingly demanding and difficult to please as they enter the devaluation phase, belittling their victims and blaming them for everything wrong in the relationship. During heated arguments, the criticism is especially noticeable, causing the victim to overapologize for things that are not their fault. Victims may believe the abuser only wants the best for them, leading to trauma bonding and making it hard to escape the narcissistic cycle.

4. Manipulation and Gaslighting

In this stage, the abusive partner distorts the truth and dismisses the victim's worries in order to deny their feelings and experiences. A narcissist's use of gaslighting can be confusing and make the victim question their own sanity. Narcissistic gaslighters will never accept responsibility for their actions and frequently point the finger at the victim. They might act composed after challenging the victim. Narcissists, sociopaths, and psychopaths are among the abusers who frequently employ gaslighting.

Unfortunately, confronting the abuser may trigger reactive abuse from the victim, leading to additional guilt and an identity crisis. Gaslighters try to keep their victims away from sources of comfort and support. Victims may experience cognitive dissonance when the abuser denies their behavior and blames them for relationship problems, leading them to question their own thoughts, memories, and experiences.

5. Resignation and Submission

Targets of abuse may resort to the "fawn" response in a trauma bond, engaging in people-pleasing and bargaining behaviors to maintain some stability in the relationship. They may be aware that they are being manipulated, but not enough to prevent them from questioning whether they are to blame for the abuser's behavior. Reasoning with a narcissistic partner is usually futile because they blame and criticize the target while shifting the argument. Targets may do things the abuser's way to avoid conflict, allowing the abuser to continue disrespecting their boundaries. Abused people may become more reliant on their abuser and fear leaving because of safety concerns, such as the abuser's potential escalation of violence if they lose control. Domestic conflicts sometimes turn violent or even fatal.

6. *Disconnection to a Sense of Self*

Setting boundaries in toxic relationships frequently leads to emotional manipulation and abusive behavior, leaving victims feeling powerless and exhausted. Their self-esteem is damaged, and they neglect their own needs in order to satisfy the needs of their partner, losing touch with their true selves.

Trauma bonding causes a progressive loss of self, resulting in pain and disconnection from the outside world. This results in the loss of many social connections. The resulting psychological destruction can be difficult because it involves the loss of a sense of identity and personal boundaries, which can lead to isolation and even suicidal thoughts. Years of emotional torture, shame, and guilt accumulate, making progress difficult. This intense mental deterioration can have a long-term impact on one's confidence and motivation.

7. *Emotional Addiction*

When you're in a relationship with a narcissist, the constant anxiety and stress raise your cortisol levels. You find it difficult to find pleasure in anything and crave relief from the pain of rejection, which can lead to a cycle of dependency similar to drug addiction. Trauma bonds can be cyclical, with the abuser occasionally apologizing and restarting the love-bombing process, reinforcing the target's reliance on the abusive cycle. Alternatively, the abuser may become avoidant and withhold love and attention in order to put the victim under pressure to apologize. To regain the abuser's favor, the victim may go to extremes, creating a false sense of control and reinforcing the notion that they are to blame.

Traits of a Healthy Relationship

Building and maintaining healthy relationships is an essential aspect of life. Not all relationships, however, are created equal, and some can be harmful, causing emotional, physical, or mental pain. It's critical to understand the signs of a healthy relationship and recognize when one becomes toxic. Mutual respect, trust, open communication, and a sense of equality characterize a healthy relationship. A toxic relationship, on the other hand, is defined by controlling and manipulative behaviors, a lack of respect and trust, constant criticism, and a sense of power imbalance. In this context, understanding the differences between healthy and toxic relationships is critical for knowing what to look for, being able to trust your own intuition, avoiding harmful patterns, and promoting healthy, supportive relationships.

In a healthy relationship, you experience personal growth and happiness. It's critical to recognize that perfection is not the goal, as everyone has ups and downs. However, there are some key indicators of a healthy relationship. Effective communication plays an important role in maintaining an open and honest dialogue. The practice of self-love is also important because it reflects on the relationship.

Let's look at some key characteristics and behaviors that contribute to a healthy relationship by encouraging growth, respect, and fulfillment:

1. **Comfortable pace:** The pace of the relationship feels enjoyable for both individuals involved in a healthy relationship. While it's natural to be excited and want to spend

a lot of time with someone when you first start seeing them, it's critical that both people agree on the pace of the relationship. Feeling rushed or overwhelmed is not part of a healthy dynamic. Open communication about expectations and progressing at a comfortable pace is essential for both individuals involved.

2. **Boundaries are honored and respected:** In a healthy relationship, both partners collaborate as a team, sharing goals and values. It entails respecting and acknowledging each other's boundaries, preferences, and personal space. Partners communicate openly, seek consent, and recognize the importance of boundaries for individual well-being and mutual respect.

3. **Trust and honesty:** There are a strong sense of assurance that your partner won't hurt you or threaten the relationship. Trust comes easily, without any doubts about intentions or loyalty. They respect your privacy and do not put you through any tests. You can be open and honest about your life and feelings without fear. While they may not always agree with what you say, their responses are thoughtful and rational, creating a safe environment for open communication.

4. **Independence and authenticity:** There is room for individuality and personal development. Outside of the relationship, both partners support each other's interests and relationships. When there is independence and freedom to be oneself, trust and honesty thrive. It also entails encouraging one another to take risks while providing a safe and accepting environment in which to be authentic and valued. Both partners have each other's backs, confronting disrespectful behavior with courage, respect, and honesty and holding each other accountable in a loving and forgiving manner.

5. **Mutual respect and equality:** Respecting each other's beliefs and opinions, as well as appreciating each other for who you are, establishes a positive foundation for the relationship. Support and celebration flourish as both partners applaud each other's accomplishments, dreams, and hard work. The relationship has a sense of balance, with both individuals putting in equal effort to ensure its success. There is no dominance of one person's preferences or opinions because each person listens to and hears the other's ideas, making compromises as needed. In a healthy relationship, you regard your own needs and interests as equally important as those of your partner. Even though each partner may invest more in their respective strengths, the outcome is always fair and equal.

6. **Accountability:** This means taking responsibility for one's actions and words, refraining from shifting blame, and admitting mistakes. Each partner in the relationship makes an effort to consider and admit any wrongdoing on their part. When this is recognized, genuine apologies are offered, along with consistent efforts to improve the relationship. It also entails acknowledging the impact of words or behavior, even if unintentional, and accepting responsibility for them.

7. **Kindness:** This is the foundation of warmth and consideration in a healthy relationship. It entails small acts that accumulate positive emotions, fueling the progression of the relationship. It can be difficult to be kind to someone we are angry with, but kindness is that much more essential in these situations. Both individuals in a healthy relationship are caring and empathetic and provide comfort and support. Kindness is reciprocated, with both partners doing things to make each other happy. It entails showing compassion and being interested in each other's problems and interests.

8. **Healthy conflict and resolution:** Conflict is dealt with openly and respectfully. It entails nonjudgmental discussions to address issues before they become more serious. It's not acceptable to yell at or belittle others. It's natural to disagree and agree to disagree on certain topics. Throughout the resolution process, healthy conflict sets appropriate expectations, promotes self-awareness, and maintains kindness and respect. Dealing with relationship conflict necessitates planning, practice, and clear communication.

9. **Fun:** Fun and enjoyment are abundant in healthy relationships. Partners strengthen their bond by sharing laughter, relaxation, and exciting adventures. Finding humor in everyday life and keeping a lighthearted attitude reduces stress, improves mood, and deepens intimacy. A fun relationship also fosters resilience and reduces conflict, resulting in an overall positive and uplifting experience. While no relationship is fun all the time, the good times should outnumber the bad, making you happy and bringing out the best in each other.

10. **Intimacy:** Couples in healthy relationships prioritize and nurture various types of intimacy. Vulnerability and sharing deep emotions, fears, and hopes to foster emotional intimacy. Intellectual intimacy entails exchanging ideas and thoughts, even when they differ. Spiritual intimacy necessitates a shared commitment to personal growth, acceptance of change, and facing challenges together. These types of intimacy assist in maintaining a strong connection and preventing the deterioration that is common in long-term relationships.

It's critical to understand how trauma bonds differ from healthy connections as we delve into the topic of trauma bonds and their impact on relationships. However, in order to fully comprehend the complexities of this dynamic, we must also understand the cycle of abuse and the reactive behaviors that perpetuate it. In the following chapter, we will look at the patterns and stages of the abusive cycle, shed light on the behaviors that keep it going, and explore the difficult journey to breaking free. Understanding these aspects is critical for those seeking healing and more fulfilling relationships.

Chapter 3:

The Cycle of Abuse—Responsive Behaviors That Perpetuate It

Individuals who are subjected to dysfunction or narcissistic abuse frequently develop coping mechanisms and responsive behaviors in order to navigate the tumultuous dynamics of their relationship. The goal of this chapter is to look closely at these common responses and see how they contribute to the cycle of abuse.

It's important to note that isolated or infrequent responses to dysfunction do not always indicate a problem. However, when these responses become ingrained coping patterns, they can unintentionally keep people trapped in a cycle of abuse and trauma bonding. The longer a person stays in a dysfunctional relationship, the more severe the damage becomes, and the long-term effects of trauma bonding become apparent.

By investigating the complexities of these responsive behaviors, we can gain a better understanding of their impact on our lives. Examining our own reactions to dysfunction and abuse provides insight into how we have adapted and survived these difficult circumstances. By illuminating these patterns, we can start to build a road map for healing and growth that will assist in navigating the path to freedom and self-empowerment.

The Cycle of Abuse

Abuse is a destructive pattern that causes deep emotional wounds in relationships. Understanding this cycle is essential for those who are caught in it, as it provides a path to healing and liberation. It penetrates various relationships and affects people from all walks of life, transcending backgrounds, social status, and personal strength. This awareness serves as a reminder to show empathy and understanding to those who have suffered. Being trapped in this cycle means constantly being vulnerable to physical, verbal, and emotional abuse, with even brief moments of calm failing to provide true peace of mind.

The beginning of a relationship is one of idealization, where a manipulative partner showers the target with love, attention, and gifts, sharing intimate secrets and weaknesses to create a deep bond. At this stage, the manipulative partner is so adept at reflecting the target's interests and values that the target feels valued and can believe they have found their soulmate. However, it is important to understand that this idealization is a calculated tactic used to set the perfect conditions for future control and exploitation.

1. Tension Buildup

A triggering event, such as problems, crises, setbacks, or misunderstandings in the abuser's life or relationship, often starts the cycle of abuse. This causes a surge of resentment within the abuser, resulting in increased tension and a variety of negative emotions. The victim is frequently blamed, worsening the situation.

As the pressure builds, you may have felt on edge, hyper-aware of their demands, oscillating between wariness and over-functioning with support. The tension eventually reaches a breaking point, increasing the possibility of various forms of abuse occurring.

2. Abuse Incidence

As the relationship becomes increasingly tense, the abuser eventually loses their cool and turns on their victim in an effort to regain control. Abuse can manifest itself in a variety of ways, including verbal, physical, and emotional abuse. It can happen in isolated incidents or over a period of days or even weeks.

Physical or sexual violence, offensive remarks, threats, manipulation, and emotional blackmail are all examples of abuse. The abuser may shift blame onto the victim, accusing them of provocation or blaming their actions for relationship problems. It is crucial to recognize that abusive behavior is a deliberate choice, and while stress may contribute, it never justifies mistreatment. Nobody deserves to be treated in this manner.

3. Reconciliation

As the tension subsides, the abuser tries to reconcile with the victim. They may make kind gestures, give gifts, and show affection to restore the relationship's previous harmony. Apologies, guilt, and remorse may be expressed, along with attempts to reestablish trust and forgiveness through charm and emotional manipulation.

This devoted behavior can cause the victim's brain to release chemicals that promote bonding and closeness, blurring the distinction between love and abuse (Raypole, 2020). The victim might let down their guard, forgiving the abuser and hoping for a better future. However, it must be recognized that this optimism tends to be misplaced within the cycle of abuse.

4. Calm Before the Storm

Following reconciliation, there is a period of tranquility and calm that sometimes exceeds previous levels of unity. Both parties frequently invent explanations or justifications to avoid confronting the painful reality of the abuse. The abusive partner will apologize while blaming others, justify their actions with external factors, deny or minimize the abuse, or accuse you of provocation. They exhibit deep remorse, a promise of change, and increased attentiveness to your needs. This reprieve alleviates the pain and tension caused by the abuse, leading you to question your perception of the severity of previous incidents.

Instances of abuse and transgression appear to be a thing of the past. The abuser may try to change their behavior and work to resolve the issues at hand. It encourages the victim of abuse to believe that things are actually improving.

However, unless the underlying issues, setbacks, or conflicts are addressed, the cycle will undoubtedly repeat. Challenges are an unavoidable part of life, and the proclivity for individuals to resort to violence as pressure mounts means that the relationship remains trapped in an abusive cycle.

This pattern of abuse minimizes the severity of the abuser's behavior, increasing the likelihood that it will occur again in the future. This creates a cycle in which the abuser can apologize and temporarily make things better. The abuse will inevitably resurface, resulting in a cycle of tension and temporary resolution.

In addition to the above cycle within the relationship, some victims also experience the below additional phases (The Editors, 2023):

5. Discard Phase

In the discard phase, the abuser abruptly ends the relationship and seeks new sources of approval and attention. If you provoke their anger or challenge their false self-image, they may discard you. Unfortunately, as you may have experienced for yourself, that doesn't necessarily mean the relationship is truly over. It's a painful pause between cycles of abuse when your abuser leaves you and seeks new sources of supply. This stage can be traumatic, leaving you feeling abandoned and confused about the future of the relationship.

6. Hoovering Phase

Following the discard stage, abused victims often undergo a manipulation stage called "hoovering." At this stage, the abuser tries to lure the victim back into the toxic relationship. This tactic involves repeating the initial idealization stage while making exaggerated gestures and promising a better future to convince the victim that the abuser has changed and is repentant. Although this manipulative behavior is repetitive and predictable, victims may rationalize abuse, focus on positive moments, and convince themselves that the relationship is satisfying. Low self-esteem can lead victims to believe they are not worth more or that no one wants them.

Breaking the cycle of abuse requires addressing the underlying cause: the abusive behavior and tendencies of the abuser (Ricee, 2022). Sadly, victims may initially blame themselves, making it difficult to break free. However, victims have the power to interrupt and escape the cycle by employing various strategies. Recognizing the pattern of abuse is the crucial first step, as it provides awareness and empowers individuals to regain control and seek a healthier path forward.

Acknowledging this reality is critical to taking in the cyclical nature of abuse and encouraging oneself to seek long-term change. It's a call to recognize that mere moments of calm cannot erase the history of abuse and that true healing necessitates addressing the root causes and breaking free from the destructive patterns that keep the cycle going.

How It Persists

People frequently remain in abusive relationships due to a variety of psychological factors. At the outset, abuse can be subtle, gradually increasing in severity over time, which can make it challenging to identify the insidiously poisonous nature of the relationship. When we are in the thick of it, trying to get by day to day, it can be difficult to see the big picture.

If we imagine experiencing the level of abuse and manipulation that occurs later in the relationship from the start, it would've been clear that leaving would be the best course of action. Toxic relationships, on the other hand, develop slowly, much like psychotherapist Heather Kent's analogy of a lobster slowly cooking in water (The Editors, 2023).

While a lobster would be more shocked and aware if directly placed in boiling water, a gradual rise in temperature would be less noticeable. Similarly, abuse in an abusive relationship typically begins slowly and escalates over time, making it difficult for the victim to recognize the danger they are in.

There are also psychological factors at work, such as attachment and emotional dependency. Victims may have formed emotional bonds with their abusers, making separation difficult. Fear of the unknown, financial dependence, low self-esteem, and the abuser's manipulation tactics all contribute to the decision to stay.

Furthermore, those who have been abused may have hope that their abuser will change or that the positive aspects of the relationship will outweigh the harm done to them. When combined with the abuser's isolation and control, this can create a sense of helplessness and make leaving appear impossible.

While counseling can be an effective tool for healing from abuse, navigating couples therapy with a narcissistic partner requires caution. Many therapists have had limited success when it comes to engaging narcissistic people and facilitating temporary changes through negotiated agreements. These agreements, however, frequently fail when the narcissistic partner is triggered, resulting in a recurring pattern of in-and-out couples' therapy. This remains the best outcome to date (Greenberg, 2019).

When dealing with a narcissistic partner, it is essential to approach couples counseling with caution. Their ability to manipulate the process and project their own problems onto their partner may hinder progress and aggravate the victim's distress. It's critical to find a skilled therapist who can see through the manipulation and provide appropriate healing support to ensure effective therapy. Furthermore, it's important to note that some religious counselors may prioritize preserving the marriage above all else, potentially impeding the victim's progress and overlooking the harmful dynamics. As a result, it is important to select a therapist who understands the complexities of an abusive relationship.

Continuous emotional and psychological abuse has far-reaching consequences for the brain, frequently resulting in trauma and long-term consequences. Traumatized people may experience hypervigilance and paralysis, making it difficult for them to flee the abusive situation. Because they are unable to engage in the typical fight or flight response, the stored stress in their bodies keeps them trapped and exhausted.

Understanding the impact of trauma is critical for breaking free from the guilt and shame associated with entering or remaining in a toxic relationship. The complex effects form strong bonds between the survivor and the abuser, making severing ties difficult. Cognitive dissonance emerges as victims try to reconcile the abusive reality with their initial impression of the abuser as a confidante and lover.

This defense mechanism, known as "abuse amnesia," allows them to cope with the trauma by denying or rationalizing the abuse. The abuse cycle's slow and insidious nature strengthens the trauma bond formed between abuser and victim, similar to Stockholm Syndrome. Trauma bonding is difficult to break, especially for those who have experienced violence or abuse in the past.

Economic dependence, cultural or religious beliefs, and concerns for the well-being of children are all practical reasons for staying in toxic relationships. Regardless of the logic of these justifications, belief in their truth has enormous power, even if it does not correspond to reality.

In some cases, people may choose to stay in toxic relationships out of fear for their safety. Exiting an abusive relationship may result in an increase in cruelty, including but not limited to stalking, physical assault, and attempts to manipulate to discourage the victim from moving on.

Abusers may use techniques such as threatening the victim, their children, or themselves, manipulating the victim's emotions, and instilling feelings of guilt or sympathy in the victim. The burden of feeling responsible for preventing impending violence may cause victims to struggle when attempting to leave an abusive relationship, especially if it is combined with emotional manipulation.

It's very important to realize that choosing to remain in these conditions does not signify weakness or a lack of willpower. Instead, it is a nuanced reaction to the victim's very real danger and fear. It frequently takes careful planning, assistance from experts or support networks, and access to resources that put the victim's safety first in order to escape such relationships.

To ensure the well-being of victims in these circumstances and give them the tools they need to break the cycle of abuse, it is crucial to be aware of the risks involved and offer them thorough assistance. Knowing these behavioral mechanisms helps us understand why people continue to stay in abusive relationships. It draws attention to the complexity of the situation and underlines how important it is to provide resources, support, and empathy in order to assist victims in ending the cycle of abuse.

Coping Mechanisms That Keep Us Stuck

When we are in a dysfunctional relationship, our survival instincts kick in, prompting us to develop coping mechanisms and responses to help us navigate the chaos and pain. We can begin to dismantle the barriers that prevent us from reclaiming our autonomy and seeking healthier, more fulfilling relationships by examining our own responses and coping patterns. While these responses may not be problematic when used infrequently or in isolation, relying on them as a pattern of coping can prolong our suffering and exacerbate the damage caused by the dysfunctional relationship.

Within the context of dysfunction and narcissistic abuse, our responses function as adaptive strategies for navigating the volatile dynamics in which we find ourselves. These reactions stem from a desire to survive and defend ourselves but they can also keep us mired in the cycle of abuse.

1. **Low self-esteem:** The relationship between self-esteem and abuse is cyclical. Low self-esteem can lead to entering abusive relationships, and the abuse reduces self-esteem even further. If you believe you are unworthy or damaged, you are likely to attract partners who will reinforce these beliefs. Low expectations, as well as comparing the relationship to worse alternatives, can make abuse appear normal or tolerable. Childhood abuse or neglect shapes our understanding of love, making it more likely that we will remain in unhealthy relationships.

2. **Power imbalance:** Victims of abuse may be hesitant to leave because of the abuser's power. This control can manifest as financial dependence, where the victim is financially dependent on the abuser, or emotional manipulation, where the victim's sense of self has been eroded, and they feel defined by the abusive relationship.

3. **Exclusively fixating on the positives while ignoring the abusive behavior:** Victims of abuse often dissociate from their traumatic experiences by avoiding discussions, suppressing emotions, and remaining hypervigilant. This emotional detachment enables them to focus on the positive aspects of their partner, resulting in a favorable perception of their positive qualities.

4. **Justifying the abusive behavior:** Victims may rationalize or blame themselves for the abuse, saying things like "It's not that bad" or "I deserved it." They may also justify the abuser's behavior by attributing it to the abuser's troubled past or emotional state, hoping that counseling will solve the problem. Gaslighting reinforces this distortion by having the abuser deny or minimize the abuse, causing the victim to doubt their own reality and internalize the lies they've been told.

5. **Always defend or justify your perspective or position:** It becomes necessary to defend your feelings or position in an abusive relationship because the abuser constantly invalidates and dismisses them. You communicate extensively, seeking validation and resolution. This includes conducting research on communication techniques, carefully selecting words, and relying on written exchanges.

6. **Covering up the abuse:** Abuse victims often hide their experiences in an effort to rationalize their actions, protect themselves from consequences, and prevent embarrassment. Trauma bonds form emotional attachments, leading them to believe they love and want to protect their abuser.

7. **Overindulging in researching their behavior and motives:** Excessive time spent researching why an abusive partner behaves the way they do, such as googling dysfunctional relationships, narcissism, and abuse, and joining online support

groups, is frequently a response to the victim's desire to understand and solve the problems in their relationship.

8. **Fear of loneliness:** Some people stay in toxic relationships because they believe it is preferable to being alone. This decision is affected by impaired judgment and low self-esteem, which lead to a fear of being on their own. By remaining, they forgo the opportunity to find a healthier and more suitable partner.

9. **Rage:** Victims may react with reactive anger, such as verbal outbursts, yelling, or expressing anger through writing. They have difficulty thinking rationally, and their anger may cloud their judgment. They might revert to complaining about the problems in-depth on social media posts or in long, irate emails with no useful purpose. This intense rage can have an effect on their overall perception of the world and their relationships.

10. **Projection onto external parties:** Because of the confusion caused by the trauma bond, victims may find themselves repeatedly complaining about the dysfunction to friends or relying on family to intervene without the true intention of ultimately leaving the situation. While it is natural to seek help without resolving and acknowledging the fundamental problems, this approach may fail to address the underlying issues and can perpetuate a cycle of venting without taking effective action.

11. **Investment:** As the level of investment in a relationship grows, so does the difficulty of ending it. Individuals are more likely to stay in a relationship that has taken a significant amount of time, effort, energy, and resources, even if it is detrimental to their overall health and well-being.

12. **The illusion of control:** Victims may delude themselves into believing they have control over the situation or have coping

mechanisms for dealing with abuse, such as ignoring or downplaying it. Though developing these defenses may seem necessary for those who choose to remain in the toxic attachment, it is crucial to accept the harsh reality and prioritize one's well-being by taking action to leave the toxic relationship.

13. **Codependent behavior:** This can take the form of enabling the abuser, prioritizing their needs, and ignoring personal boundaries. Victims frequently believe they are responsible for the abuser's actions and that their love can change them. They may engage in caregiving behaviors, perpetuating an emotionally entangled cycle that makes it difficult for them to leave the relationship.

14. **Attempting to appease:** Victims of abuse may believe that pleasing the abuser will prevent escalation or may genuinely want to please them because of the benefits they have received. Dopamine and oxytocin are hormones that play a role in creating a distorted reward system and forming trauma bonds that override negative feelings caused by abuse.

15. **Family and children:** Staying in a toxic relationship for the sake of children was common in the past, and it still happens today. On the other hand, the belief that children are better off witnessing abuse than experiencing parental separation is a contorted sentiment. You teach your children that enduring pain and abuse is preferable to letting go and staying.

16. **Common beliefs about love and relationships:** Our choices are influenced by dysfunctional beliefs about love, relationships, and self-worth. People in unhealthy relationships may believe that all relationships bring pain, that love is meant to hurt, that enduring pain is acceptable in love, and that they are unworthy of happiness or satisfying relationships. These beliefs keep them in unhealthy relationships and make it difficult for them to seek healthier alternatives.

17. **Engaging in substance abuse:** Victims of abuse may turn to substance abuse to cope with the trauma inflicted on them. Alcohol, sleeping pills, and prescription drugs provide temporary relief and an escape from the unbearable pain. However, this coping mechanism can lead to dependency, making it more difficult to leave an abusive relationship.

18. **Feeling trapped and unable to leave:** Victims are discouraged from leaving abusive relationships because they are afraid of physical violence. Leaving increases the likelihood of harm, and abusers may target those who intervene. According to research, a significant number of domestic violence-related homicides involve people other than the initial victim, such as family members, new partners, friends, or law enforcement officers who try to help (Smith et al., 2014). Many people are reluctant to leave violent situations due to their fear of the violence intensifying.

19. **Isolation:** Abusers isolate victims from their support network while making themselves the sole source of trust. In a vulnerable state, the victim cuts ties with caring people who could help. With fewer people around, reminders of the abuse's unacceptability fade, further entangling the victim in the abusive dynamic.

The longer we stay in a dysfunctional relationship, the more serious the consequences become. As the cycle of abuse continues, the bonds of trauma strengthen, forming what is known as a trauma bond. This bond can keep us emotionally and psychologically attached to the abuser, making breaking free from the toxic cycle extremely difficult. The stronger the trauma bond, the more difficult it is to imagine a life beyond the abuse, trapping us in an apparently never-ending cycle of pain and suffering.

We have the ability to break the cycle of abuse and trauma bonding through self-reflection, self-compassion, and understanding. We can gradually break free from the bonds of dysfunction and cultivate a life marked by self-empowerment, resilience, and the restoration of our well-being by recognizing the impact of our responses and embracing the journey of healing.

You may have gained some clarity after reflecting on your past experiences and recognizing patterns in abusive relationships, which may have helped you feel validated and less alone. And even if it didn't, that is okay too. It's important to recognize that no one deserves to be in such a situation and that there are a variety of reasons why people become involved in these types of relationships. It is essential to recognize that many people become entangled in this complex web through no fault of their own.

The following chapter will concentrate on reclaiming a sense of safety and continuing the journey from victim to survivor. One of the most important steps in achieving this is setting clear boundaries and creating a safe environment for your own recovery. You can begin the process of healing and personal growth by taking proactive and empowering steps.

Chapter 4:

Reclaiming Safety—Healing After Abuse

Reclaiming a sense of safety becomes a critical task on the path to healing after abuse. Whether the abuse was physical, emotional, or a combination of the two, the violation of personal boundaries leaves permanent scars that necessitate careful care and attention. This chapter will discuss the significance of establishing and maintaining physical and emotional boundaries as a critical step in the healing process following trauma.

Boundaries protect our physical and emotional well-being by acting as protective barriers. They serve as barriers against further harm, allowing us to regain control of our lives. Boundaries are especially important in the context of abuse because they help us create a space where we can begin to rebuild our shattered selves.

This chapter will examine different facets of boundaries and how they can be applied to various relationships in a healthy way, serving as a foundation for healing and reclaiming your sense of security and independence.

Importance of Boundaries for Healing After Trauma

Boundaries play a vital role in our lives, functioning as the line of separation between ourselves and others. They offer us a straightforward understanding of who we are and allow us to achieve equilibrium and a sense of safety. These boundaries may change and evolve along with us as we progress personally. In the context of trauma recovery, boundaries are extremely important for two main reasons: They increase feelings of security and self-worth.

In the aftermath of a traumatic event, people often feel less secure, stable, and safe, especially when reminded of their trauma. Setting boundaries allows you to feel safe, even in stressful circumstances. People recovering from trauma can get the support and understanding they need by being clear about what they need from those around them.

Furthermore, boundaries help trauma survivors regain their sense of worth. Because trauma frequently involves transgressions of our physical, intellectual, emotional, and spiritual boundaries, it can have a significant impact on how we view ourselves. This can cause insecurities and a feeling of unworthiness. Setting and upholding healthy boundaries in these areas can support personal value affirmation and confidence building.

As we embark on the journey of healing and personal growth, it's critical that we understand the significance of turning inward and prioritizing our own needs and well-being. The shift in focus emphasizes the significance of setting and maintaining personal boundaries for our general functioning and fulfillment, which is in line with the fundamental principles shown in Maslow's hierarchy of needs. Instead of compromising our boundaries to appease or accommodate others, these boundaries allow us to create space for us to attend to our own safety and basic needs first before reaching out to others. By doing so, we not only protect our well-being but also strengthen our capacity to help others rather than hinder it.

When co-parenting with an abuser, setting boundaries becomes even more challenging but equally important, if not more so. It involves navigating the difficulties of setting boundaries and security measures that safeguard our kids and us while fostering their well-being. In order to regain control over our lives and rediscover a sense of empowerment, it's also crucial to set boundaries with our family and friends, protect our financial security, and guarantee our emotional and physical safety. Boundary-setting exercises help us actively create the space needed for development, self-care, and the growth of healthier relationships.

The process of reclaiming safety through boundaries requires us to free ourselves from the negative attitudes, behaviors, and manipulation of our abusers. By setting up unbreakable boundaries, we make room for a new reality based on honesty and self-preservation. It's important to recognize the facets of life we have control over, such as how we think, our mindset, responses, language, and mannerisms. On the other hand, we must be aware of the limitations of controlling the beliefs, attitudes, actions, and decisions of others. Instead of pursuing justice for the wrongdoings of our abusers, we should put more effort into nurturing and safeguarding our own mental health and well-being.

The process of healing requires us to take control of our personal space. Our homes should be safe havens where we can feel comfortable and secure. This entails setting boundaries for our personal space, defining what is expected of others' behavior, and upholding those rules. Even when co-parenting with an abuser is required, it's crucial to reclaim our power and make sure they're not permitted in our homes. A sense of security and control can be increased by switching to smart keyless locks, installing security cameras, and changing locks.

Another way to establish our boundaries is by creating a personal space that reflects our preferences and sense of style. Decluttering and organizing our external environment can reflect how we are feeling internally and promote calm and clarity. By creating a calming environment, including music, calming colors, scented candles, or aromatherapy, and designating specific furniture for relaxation, we can reclaim our personal space as our own. This can be anything that helps you feel calm and at peace.

As we proceed along this path, it's vital that we cultivate connections that respect our boundaries. By settling into a community of people who value and respect our independence and need for privacy, we can find the encouragement and validation we need to move through the healing process. By restoring our sense of safety through boundary-setting, we make significant strides toward recovering from abuse and reclaiming our sense of self-worth and empowerment.

Boundary Setting Basics

Although it can be complicated, establishing, and upholding boundaries is a crucial skill for trauma survivors on the road to recovery. Working on boundary setting takes up a lot of time in therapy because it can relieve stress while also offering a sense of freedom. Therapy can be an excellent resource if you're trying to improve this skill.

Here are a few fundamental measures to help you establish and uphold healthy boundaries:

1. **Take baby steps:** It can be overwhelming to begin setting boundaries with everyone in your life at once. Start by establishing a few relatively small boundaries. If your sibling frequently disrupts your alone time by showing up unexpectedly, politely request that they give you a heads-up or set specific times that work for you. If someone consistently questions or criticizes your beliefs, let them know that you would appreciate their respect for your point of view and avoid emotionally draining discussions. If you feel pressed to attend social gatherings you don't want to attend, practice politely declining invitations that don't match your preferences or values. Put your health first and attend events that truly bring you joy. By beginning small, you can gradually build up your confidence in setting boundaries.

2. **Be consistent:** Once you've set a boundary, try to stick to it as much as possible. Boundaries are allowed to shift and evolve but keep in mind that these shifts should reflect your own needs and values, not those of others. If you can't keep them up at first, be gentle with yourself. All good habits need practice. Try again, be persistent, and have faith in yourself.

Consistency strengthens your boundaries and aids others in understanding and respecting them.

3. **Begin at home:** If you aren't ready to set boundaries with others, start with personal boundaries. Determine which aspects of your life need to be more strictly regulated. If you want to spend less time on social media, for example, start by limiting your daily usage. If you feel the need for more downtime, set up a personal space in your home where you can unwind, reflect, or engage in activities without interruptions. When a friend asks for help with a problem that at the time seems overwhelming, give yourself the grace to respond when you're in a more open and receptive frame of mind. Setting boundaries with yourself allows you to reap the benefits while remaining safe, fostering increased confidence.

4. **Communicate:** Even after you've established a boundary, communicate, and affirm it as often as necessary. This ongoing communication ensures that everyone involved is aware of your boundaries. If your boundaries are shifting, be transparent about the reasons for the changes. Effective communication aids in the preservation of clarity and mutual understanding.

Remember that setting and maintaining boundaries is a process that takes time and reflection. Be kind to yourself and acknowledge your achievements along the way. By practicing this essential ability, you empower yourself to create a safe and nurturing environment that respects your needs and values.

Boundaries With Your Abusive Ex

Even the notion of setting boundaries with an abusive ex can feel very challenging and daunting. Establishing boundaries in the aftermath of an abusive relationship can be confusing and emotionally draining. It's difficult to set clear boundaries when dealing with someone who has previously ignored your well-being. However, it's important that you navigate through these uncomfortable feelings because these boundaries are critical for your health and healing. Remember, you have the right to create an environment in which your needs and well-being are met.

Physical Boundaries

1. **Establish a 'no contact' rule:** Establish a strict boundary of no contact with your abusive ex in order to make room for your protection and healing. This involves steering clear of conversations over the phone, text messages, and in-person meetings.

2. **Restricted access:** Change the locks on your doors, install security systems, or, if necessary, take legal action to restrict or eliminate your ex's access to your physical space.

3. **Public interaction:** Establish a rule that you will only speak with your ex in public or in the presence of a reliable third party in order to protect your safety and avoid any potential manipulation or abuse.

Emotional Boundaries

4. **Give yourself the green light to rethink your boundaries:** As you heal and reclaim your sense of safety and control, be aware that your boundaries may need to change over time.

5. **Keep communication simple, direct, and short:** If communication with your abusive ex is unavoidable, set a boundary to keep interactions brief, direct, and focused solely on necessary matters. Avoid long discussions or disclosing personal information that could be used against you.

6. **No emotional manipulation:** Set a boundary that prohibits you from engaging in any form of emotional manipulation, such as guilt-tripping, gaslighting, or attempting to control your emotions or decisions.

Other Boundaries Concerning Safety

1. Block your ex on social media platforms to keep them from seeing your personal information and protect your privacy.

2. Whenever a situation calls for it, always take screenshots of any harassing or threatening texts as evidence.

3. Keep a stalking log to document any incidents or behaviors that may endanger your safety.

4. Consider spending a short time with a dependable friend or family member if you feel unsafe.

5. If necessary, report the incident to the police or request a protective order to have your ex's access to any weapons taken away and to bolster your legal protection.

Always keep in mind that these boundaries are essential for your safety and well-being. To ensure your protection, modify and adapt them in accordance with your particular circumstances and seek advice from experts, such as counselors or legal authorities.

Boundaries When You Need to Co-parent With an Abuser

After leaving an abusive relationship, co-parenting presents particular difficulties and safety concerns. Even though co-parenting has its share of challenges, dealing with an ex-spouse who has a history of abuse calls for additional consideration. Your primary concern should be making sure you and your kids are safe. Co-parenting with an abusive ex-spouse is possible with the right planning and by taking the necessary precautions to address any challenges or safety concerns that may arise.

It might not come easy, but it is possible:

1. **Clear rules for communication:** Use written correspondence (email or texts) to establish a record and avoid distortion. Avoid personal attacks and keep the conversation focused on the kids. For safe and irreversible communication, think about using online scheduling tools like Family Wizard.

2. **Seek guidance from impartial parties:** To reduce harmful or controlling behaviors, have a neutral mediator present during communication, whether it be in person or through another channel. Use supportive friends, family, or psychologists to express and process your emotions.

3. **Establish a separation protocol:** Set up a clear visitation schedule that prevents miscommunication or manipulation. As a precaution for your own safety, insist on public areas for drop-offs and pick-ups. Engage the legal system to have a court-ordered plan created if an agreement cannot be reached (Lambert, 2022).

4. **Maintain the visitation routine:** Both parents must adhere to the agreed-upon schedule. Expect the abusive parent to make an effort to change, refuse to comply, or harass the other parent. In order to uphold the agreement, it becomes essential to establish clear boundaries and limits.

5. **Use an independent location for pick-ups and drop-offs:** To ensure safety during exchanges and lessen exposure to abusive behavior, choose a public setting like a police station, restaurant parking lot, or other open areas.

6. **The steady increase in co-parenting time:** Work with a mediator to develop a step-by-step plan where the abusive parent gradually gains more time with the children as they go through therapy or counseling if immediate co-parenting is not safe (Fagan, 2022).

7. **Clearly outline periods of possession:** Indicate the number of days the child will spend with each parent each week, month, and year. Include plans for the child's school years, summer breaks, and holidays.

8. **Set limitations on holidays:** Establish precise rules for the start and end of periods of possession, as well as for drop-offs and pick-ups. Clarify specifics in court orders to prevent misunderstandings and ease tension during the holidays.

9. **Parallel parenting:** Make daily decisions for the kids alone rather than fully co-parenting, and only consult with the ex-spouse about important choices like the kids' schools. Recognize that you don't need to like your co-parent as long as they follow the court's order and keep you and your children safe (Crawshaw, 2018).

10. **Keep a record of everything:** Even if it has been a while since the separation, keep a record of your ex-spouse's actions and behaviors. This documentation may be helpful in upcoming legal proceedings but refrain from questioning your kids in a cross-examination.

11. **Identify and define the distinction:** To safeguard your child's well-being, make a distinction between simply bothersome behavior and potentially harmful behavior. When setting boundaries, keep conflicts to a minimum unless your child is in immediate danger.

12. **Identify the means of communication:** To maintain boundaries and ensure effective communication, work with

your co-parent to establish preferred communication channels, such as set times for phone calls or email correspondence.

The journey is sure to be filled with its fair share of difficulties and stress in the complicated world of co-parenting, whether with a supportive ex-partner or a toxic one. There are, however, ways to lighten the load and encourage a healthier environment for both you and your child. You can navigate this path with greater resilience and foster a more fulfilling co-parenting experience by remaining civil, placing your well-being and the well-being of your child first, and asking for help when necessary. Remember that you are not alone and that you can overcome obstacles and create a nurturing environment for your child's development and happiness.

Boundaries With Family and Friends

Establishing boundaries after leaving an abusive relationship doesn't stop with your abusive ex. They're needed, even with your family and friends. It's important to understand that they may not entirely understand your experiences or feelings. As you go through the healing process, establishing clear boundaries that protect your well-being and foster a positive environment becomes even more crucial:

1. **Respecting your privacy:** Ask your friends and family to be considerate of your need for privacy and personal space. Inform them that you value their concern but would prefer to keep some aspects of your life private.

2. **Limiting conversations about your past:** Ask loved ones to refrain from bringing up your previous abusive relationship unless you bring it up yourself. Communicate how going back to those memories could be upsetting and interfere with your healing.

3. **Supporting your decisions:** Make it clear that you require their assistance as you embark on a healing and life-building

journey. Even if they don't fully understand your decisions, ask them to respect and honor them.

4. **Keeping an open mind:** Ask your loved ones to refrain from criticizing your choices or behavior. Describe how you require a welcoming environment where you can feel secure and accepted.

5. **Limiting unsolicited advice:** Unknowingly, your loved ones may become overly invested in your situation, which can get overwhelming. Communicate to them that while you value their concern, you would prefer to seek counsel or direction when you are ready. Request that they respect your independence and refrain from making uninvited suggestions.

6. **Knowing your triggers:** Inform your close circle of particular triggers that might result in anxiety or emotional distress. In order to avoid or reduce those triggers during interactions, gently ask for their understanding and sensitivity.

7. **Communicating openly and truthfully:** Encourage your friends and family to communicate honestly and openly. Let them know that you value their support and would be grateful if they could do so by being respectful and understanding when they express their thoughts and concerns.

It's essential for your friends and family to understand your boundaries, emotions, and healing needs as you reclaim your space after leaving an abusive relationship. The right people will respect and support these boundaries because they recognize the importance of your well-being. Remember that those who struggle with your boundaries are often the ones who benefit from your lack of them. By establishing and maintaining healthy boundaries, you create a space for healing and genuine connections to thrive.

Financial Boundaries

A safety plan is necessary to protect yourself and create an emergency action plan. Begin by identifying a reliable support network and a safe location to escape to if necessary. For added security, consider installing a security system and changing the locks.

Before you address your finances, you must first create a safe environment. Separate yourself from your ex-partner and, if necessary, consider relocating. Don't let financial concerns keep you from becoming a homeowner. Many locations offer government-backed financial and housing options with lower credit score requirements, making them available to people with challenging credit histories. Distancing yourself physically is essential for your well-being and a fresh start:

1. **Set up a bank account and begin saving:** Choose a reputable bank that meets your needs. Consider online options or credit unions in your area. Investigate fees and services to make an informed decision.

2. **Set up a budget:** Sort through your bills to see how much you can save each month. Use online budget templates to track your income and expenses, or create your own. Determine where you can cut back and save money.

3. **Reduce unnecessary spending:** Cut back on variable expenses such as unused streaming services, dining out, and emotional spending. Examine your finances and eliminate unnecessary charges. Set an intention to stick to the limits you've established.

4. **Create an emergency fund:** Set aside money for unanticipated medical, childcare, legal, or safety expenses. Save as much as

you can and think about opening a high-yield savings account. Contribute on a regular basis to alleviate financial stress.

5. **Take care of your debt:** Make a plan to pay off your debts, beginning with the smallest. Prioritize debt repayment while meeting basic needs. Seek professional guidance if necessary.

6. **Consult a financial advisor:** Find a professional to help you manage your finances and plan for the future. Choose an advisor who understands your requirements and can assist you in developing a tailored strategy.

7. **Set targets:** Even small goals can drive you. Aim to pay off a portion of your debt, set up a vacation fund, increase your retirement contributions, or save for a down payment on a house. Each goal contributes to your long-term happiness.

8. **Don't forget your resources:** Seek help from a trusted support system and consider counseling to aid in your healing process. Counseling can provide you with useful tools and approaches to help you recover.

Regardless of the difficulties you face, keep in mind that there is hope and support available to you. Regardless of how overwhelmed you feel, know that there's an end to the darkness and that you are not alone.

Addressing financial stress and seeking professional assistance can help you on your healing journey. By learning how to navigate your financial situation and seeking the assistance you require, you will be one step closer to healing.

Remember that you have the inner strength to overcome your obstacles and create a brighter future. That strength lies in reaching out for help, being kind to yourself, remaining resilient, and seizing the opportunities for growth and healing that await you.

Personal Boundaries

Being in a toxic relationship after long-term emotional abuse can impair our ability to recognize when we're being used, manipulated, or taken for granted. Even when we are aware of it, self-doubt creeps in and causes us to question our own perceptions. Unfortunately, emotional abusers and manipulators exist in our world, and when our boundaries are breached, we become ideal targets for their tactics. It's critical to recognize that this pattern provides a chance for self-healing and growth.

Developing and enforcing healthy personal boundaries is an important part of the healing process because it allows you to reclaim your sense of self and establish emotional safety. By establishing boundaries, you can restore your self-confidence, trust in yourself, and self-worth:

1. **Identify your values:** Reexamine your values to build a solid basis for establishing boundaries that reflect your principles and ideals.

2. **Eliminate triggers:** Remove any visual reminders of that abusive connection from your environment, even if it takes some time to fully let go. Remove the images, block the abuser on social media, and close shared accounts.

3. **Renew your home:** To establish a new and empowering environment, swap out anything that makes you think of the abuser for brand-new, uniquely your items.

4. **Remove sensory triggers:** Reduce or get rid of smells and sounds that bring back unpleasant memories. Manage what you can while practicing and assigning new responses for triggers that cannot be avoided.

5. **Recognize your needs:** Acknowledge and prioritize your own needs first while letting go of guilt and the tendency to put others' needs first. Take care of your physical, mental, emotional, and spiritual well-being on a regular basis.

6. **Allow yourself to say "no":** Embrace the ability to say "no" with the intention of protecting your boundaries and let go of your guilt. Keep in mind that healthy boundaries are respected and allowed in healthy relationships.

7. **See it through:** Maintain your boundaries, even if it is uncomfortable or frightening. As you rebuild your boundaries and sense of self, be consistent and patient with yourself.

8. **Rewrite the narrative:** Reclaim your thoughts and spaces by rewriting your inner story. Believe in your own power and ability to live a life of self-love and reclaim your identity.

Remember that you have the ability to reclaim the spaces that were once yours. Although it may seem difficult right now, I assure you that you have the strength to make it happen. After giving so much of your life to someone who was unable to appreciate it and thus did not deserve it, you have earned the right to now take back ownership of your life. Embrace your big heart and channel that love towards yourself for a change. Believe in yourself and have faith that better days are ahead. You have the ability to write a new story full of self-empowerment and personal growth.

Being Alone

Survivors of abusive relationships may feel compelled to seek out another relationship in order to alleviate their suffering. This, however, frequently leads to them falling into the arms of another emotional predator, exacerbating their abandonment wounds. On the other hand, survivors may unintentionally push away healthy relationships due to unresolved trauma.

Regardless of whether or not one intends to pursue another relationship, it helps to spend time alone in order to heal. This break allows the cycle of abuse to be interrupted and broken, which is especially important for survivors of childhood abuse or those who have a history of unhealthy relationships. You can experience a renewed sense of a healthier self by embracing the idea of being single.

Despite societal standards for relationships, being single can be a valuable experience, especially for trauma survivors. According to studies, single people have the same capacity for happiness as those in relationships (DePaulo, 2007; Grime et al., 2015).

During this trying time in your life, it's critical to accept and work through your emotions. Allow yourself to fully feel and express yourself without unconsciously masking it with distractions. Lean on your trusted circles for support and accept loneliness as a legitimate and valid emotion. The intensity of the pain will fade over time, allowing you to achieve a state of calm and clarity.

Prioritize listening to your own needs and preferences. Respect your personal pace and comfort zone by only taking advice that truly resonates with you. Recognize that there is nothing wrong with your current situation and embrace the freedom and self-awareness that come with being alone.

Being single allows you to forge a new normal that prioritizes healing and self-sufficiency. It provides an opportunity to set higher standards for future relationships by nurturing connections that uplift and support while filtering out toxic influences. Furthermore, being single allows you to grieve and process complex emotions without accidentally projecting them onto others.

After leaving a toxic relationship, redirecting previously expended energy and resources toward personal growth, self-care, and pursuing one's dreams becomes increasingly important. You can improve your life and reinforce your sense of wholeness and self-reliance by investing in yourself.

Staying single not only allows for personal development but can also help strengthen resistance to abusive tactics. Individuals become more sensitive to their inner voice as they heal and set boundaries, trusting their instincts, and validating their self-worth. The resulting newfound confidence acts as a shield against manipulative tactics, making it easier to identify toxic people and set healthy boundaries.

It's important to note that when discussing the significance of being single, I am not implying that remaining single forever is the ultimate goal, or that it is preferable to being in a relationship. Instead, the emphasis is on realizing that there is nothing wrong with being alone and that one can find happiness and fulfillment in solitude just as much as in a partnership. Taking time to be alone is an important step in the healing process for survivors of abuse. It enables them to accept themselves, process their trauma, and embark on a journey of self-discovery and healing. By devoting this time to their own well-being, survivors can lay a solid foundation for future relationships based on self-love, self-awareness, and a better understanding of their own needs and boundaries. Being single can be a powerful and transformative part of the journey to healing and readiness for another relationship.

While the road ahead may be bumpy, it will undoubtedly be a genuine and liberating experience. It's important to remember that the ability to save oneself lies within. Make the most of your time alone by resting, reflecting on personal desires, and making your dreams a reality.

By establishing boundaries, we are not erecting walls or shutting people out; rather, we are showing our loved ones where the door to our hearts and lives truly is. Boundaries can help us rebuild trust and restore our sense of security by acting as a powerful tool for creating a safe and nurturing environment.

Consider what you've learned in this chapter, particularly the importance of honoring our boundaries and recognizing their transformative impact on our healing journey. Boundaries allow us to define our personal limits, protect our emotional well-being, and move forward with healthier relationships. By establishing boundaries, we communicate our needs, desires, and expectations, thereby creating an environment in which we can thrive and feel respected.

With this knowledge, we will now delve deeper into financial recovery. Many survivors of abusive relationships have experienced financial dependency and abuse, putting them in a vulnerable position. It is critical that we regain control of our finances, assess our situation, and devise a strategy for achieving financial security.

In the following chapter, we will investigate the steps required to comprehend our financial situation, examine financial data, and chart a course toward financial stability. We can reclaim our sense of security and freedom by arming ourselves with the knowledge and tools needed to rebuild our financial independence.

Chapter 5:

Financial Recovery—Rebuilding Security and Freedom

Along with the emotional scars left by an abusive relationship, survivors frequently face the harsh reality of financial hardship, exacerbating the difficulties they must overcome. The aftereffects of an abusive relationship can last for a long time, affecting not only one's sense of self but also one's financial stability.

When we talk about financial recovery, we don't just mean the restoration of monetary resources. It refers to a broader process that entails understanding and reshaping one's relationship with money, removing the constraints imposed by the past, and charting a course toward a more secure and self-determined future. It is about gaining the knowledge, skills, and resilience to confidently navigate the financial landscape and reclaim control over one's own destiny.

To begin the process of financial recovery, one must first face the reality of their current financial situation. This necessitates a thorough examination of one's financial situation, including everything from income and expenses to debts and assets. By honestly assessing their financial situation, survivors gain a clear understanding of the challenges they face and can begin to devise a strategy to overcome them.

On this journey, data becomes a powerful ally. By carefully examining financial records, statements, and documentation, you can find trends, spot vulnerable areas, and pinpoint opportunities for improvement. This thorough examination serves as a foundation for making informed decisions and charting a course toward a more stable and prosperous future.

Financial recovery also necessitates taking action sooner rather than later. It's easy to put off dealing with financial issues because they're complicated or because you're afraid of making mistakes. Delaying action, on the contrary, only serves to prolong the cycle of financial distress. You can gradually regain control over your financial well-being by taking proactive steps to address immediate concerns and make necessary adjustments.

It's critical to remember that financial recovery is a time-consuming and labor-intensive process. It's a testament to the strength and determination of those who refuse to let their past define their future. Survivors can embrace newfound empowerment, break free from the bonds of abuse, and step into a brighter and more promising future by delving into the complex world of finances.

Financial Abuse and Stress

The effects of an abusive relationship permeate every aspect of a person's life and go far beyond emotional damage. Financial abuse is one of the most pernicious forms of abuse, causing significant harm to a survivor's security and future freedom. Whether the abusive partner is wealthy, vengeful, or both, they may go to extremes to exploit and manipulate the survivor's financial resources, rendering them vulnerable and deficient.

Financial abuse manifests itself in a variety of ways, each designed to exert control and cause harm. Joint accounts turn into a battleground where funds are clandestinely withdrawn, effectively removing them from the survivor's grasp. Lying by omission becomes a weapon when information about pensions or rightful entitlements is withheld. Marital assets are hidden by transferring them to a third party, exacerbating the survivor's financial insecurity.

The abuser's tactics know no bounds, even when it comes to children. They attempt to change child support in their favor by manipulating custody arrangements, lavishing the children with excessive gifts or trips, and undermining the co-parent. In some states, even if the lower-earning co-parent has sole physical custody, the abuser can take advantage of the situation, regardless of their own substantial income. This creates an ideal environment for a vindictive narcissist to thrive, as they typically hire an attorney who shares their values and files frivolous motions at the expense of the victim. Such tactics force the survivor to bear the financial burden of defending themselves or becoming embroiled in a protracted court battle, adding tremendous stress and anguish to their already burdened existence.

The trauma of abuse, combined with the subsequent financial difficulties, creates a perfect storm of stress for survivors to deal with. Stress symptoms such as depression, loss of appetite, sleep disturbances, and weight fluctuations become common companions for those who have been abused. However, these general stressors are exacerbated by the specific challenges survivors face in rebuilding their financial lives, resulting in a distinct type of suffering that is inextricably linked to money.

As survivors' journey through the difficult process of healing and recovery, it becomes critical to address the deep-seated financial stress caused by abusive relationships. This necessitates not only recognizing the various types of financial abuse but also developing strategies and support systems to reestablish financial stability and regain control over one's life. We can begin to explore effective pathways to financial recovery, laying the groundwork for a brighter and more secure future by shedding light on the far-reaching impact of financial abuse and acknowledging the specific challenges we face in the aftermath.

Assess Your Finances—Focus on the Data

Taking stock of your financial situation is an important step toward regaining your security and freedom after leaving an abusive relationship. You can gain a clear understanding of your current financial situation and make informed decisions to improve it by assessing your finances and focusing on data. Here are some steps to help you through this process:

1. Know Your Credit Score

To check your credit score, contact your bank, financial institution, or credit card company. Maintaining a good credit rating is critical because it allows you to access credit cards, rent or buy housing, buy cars, and potentially increase your income. Understanding your credit score allows you to assess your financial situation and identify areas for growth.

2. Create a Comprehensive Budget

Make a detailed budget that includes updated and specific values for all of your assets and liabilities. Assets are anything that generates income or adds value, including money in bank accounts, retirement accounts, the market value of your home, ownership interests in businesses, and future assets like a pension. Liabilities, on the other hand, are expenses or payments made to someone else, such as mortgages or rent, utilities, vehicle loans, insurance coverage, taxes, and personal maintenance such as hair, clothes, gym memberships, travel, and entertainment. A detailed budget provides you with a complete picture of your financial situation.

When it comes to budgeting, it's critical to find a method that works for your specific financial goals and circumstances. Fortunately, you can experiment with different techniques to see what works best for you. Below are a few recommendations provided by Donald Owsley (2018):

    a. *50/30/20 budget:*

        This is a popular approach to personal finance management. It entails categorizing your take-home pay into three categories: essentials, wants, and savings. The basic idea is to devote 50% of your budget to essentials, which include necessities such as housing, transportation, and bills. The remaining 30% would be allocated to wants, which include discretionary expenses such as dining out, entertainment, and hobbies. The remaining 20% should be set aside for savings, such as an emergency fund, a retirement fund, or other financial objectives. This method provides a clear and balanced framework for managing your income, ensuring that you're covering your essential expenses, enjoying some discretionary spending, and saving for the future.

b. *The 80/20 budget*

This can be considered a simplified version of the 50/30/20 budget, in which you set aside 20% of your income for savings and have the remaining 80% to spend on whatever you want. This strategy allows you to focus on saving enough money to meet your financial goals while still having enough money to cover other expenses and indulge in discretionary spending. Depending on your savings goals and financial situation, you may choose to increase or decrease the percentage set aside for savings. This method is flexible and can be a good starting point for those looking to simplify their budgeting process and save more money.

c. *Envelope method:*

This is a hands-on, visual approach to budgeting. To begin, label individual envelopes with various expense categories such as essentials, wants, and savings. You can also label more specific categories, such as rent, utilities, groceries, and pleasure. Then, for the month, decide how much you want to allocate to each category and place that amount in each corresponding envelope. The goal is to have a visual reminder of your budgeting objectives and allocations. While keeping your money in a bank is generally safer, the envelope method can help you stay on track with your budget and limit overspending.

You can use technology to your advantage by using budgeting apps that are readily available on smartphones and tablets. These apps allow you to connect your bank accounts and credit cards, allowing you to track your bills, create budgets, develop spending strategies, and more. These apps not only provide an easy way to keep track of your financial transactions, but they also allow you to set financial goals and gain valuable insights into your spending habits. Budgeting apps, with their user-friendly features, can help you manage your finances more efficiently and achieve your financial goals.

3. *Calculate Your Debt-To-Income Ratio*

Based on the information in your budget, evaluate your needs. If your liabilities exceed your assets, you should prioritize debt reduction and asset growth. Calculating your debt-to-income ratio gives you a clear picture of how much of your income goes toward debt repayment. This data assists you in evaluating your financial obligations and making the necessary changes to improve your financial stability.

By thoroughly analyzing your finances and focusing on data, you can gain valuable insights into your financial strengths and weaknesses. This information enables you to make more informed decisions and take targeted actions to reduce debt, increase assets, and improve your overall financial well-being. Remember that the road to financial recovery may be long, but with perseverance and a clear understanding of your financial situation, you can gradually rebuild your security and regain the freedom you deserve.

Take Action—Sooner Than Later

When it comes to ensuring your financial independence, having a sound plan in place is essential. You can take the necessary actions to move toward a more prosperous financial future by keeping an open mind and considering all of your options. The following are some practical ideas to think about:

1. Open a Bank Account and Begin Saving

Opening your own bank account is a critical step toward financial independence. Investigate reputable banks that meet your requirements and provide services such as in-person budgeting assistance or online financial management tools. Check to see if there are any additional fees. When opening an account, try to open one with both a checking and a savings account. Begin saving by putting aside a portion of each paycheck, even if it's only a small amount at first. Prioritize the creation of an emergency fund capable of covering essential expenses for at least three to six months. After you've done that, think about saving for other financial goals or investing for retirement.

2. Create a Strategy for Dealing With Credit Card Debt

If you are saddled with credit card debt, developing a repayment strategy is crucial. Consider balance transfer credit cards that provide an interest-free period, giving you time to regain stability without incurring additional interest charges. Investigate options that are appropriate for your credit score, as there are balance transfer cards that work for a variety of credit situations. Debt consolidation loans can also be used to consolidate multiple debts into a single, manageable payment. Before making a decision, compare interest rates and associated fees.

3. Improve Your Credit Score

A high credit score is required to obtain loans, mortgages, and favorable credit terms. Building credit can be accomplished through a variety of means, such as taking out a personal loan or making regular car payments. Applying for a credit card is one of the most straightforward ways to build credit. Choose a card with no annual fee, spend within your means, and set up automatic monthly full-balance payments. Paying off your balance in full saves you money and helps you build a good credit history. Secured credit cards, which require a deposit that serves as your credit limit, can be a viable option for those starting out with no credit history (Little and Egan, 2023).

Other measures to consider:

- Determine where you can cut costs and reduce liabilities. Examine the costs of insurance, luxury items, travel expenses, and entertainment. Be willing to replace costly items with less expensive alternatives.

- Consider how you can increase your assets. Investigate opportunities for higher-paying work, side jobs, starting a business, or making changes to your living situation.

- Examine your living situation and think about ways to cut costs or generate income. Finding roommates, moving to a more affordable location, renting out a room, or refinancing can all have a positive impact on your financial situation.

- Seek advice from an objective financial advisor who is licensed and charges by the hour to help you navigate your unique financial circumstances. It is critical to work with someone who is looking out for your best interests and can provide unbiased advice free of any potential sales agendas.

- To fully understand your financial situation and future goals, get a second opinion from another financial advisor.

- Prioritize your changes based on what requires immediate intervention and what can be dealt with gradually.

Remember that acting ahead of time is critical for financial independence. You can set yourself up for a more secure and prosperous future by following these steps and tailoring them to your specific situation. Maintain your determination, focus, and faith in your ability to achieve financial freedom.

It's made clear that creating financial security by recognizing and controlling our finances is critical. We take proactive steps toward regaining control and independence by reviewing our financial data and developing a plan.

As we move on to the next chapter, let us turn our attention to what is arguably one of the most important aspects of our healing journey: welcoming happiness and committing to positive transformation. It's time to assess what truly brings us joy and peace. We'll look back at the activities and experiences that used to make us happy and discover new ones. We will also evaluate our healthy relationships and identify the positive connections that support our well-being.

We'll explore the transformative power of opening ourselves up to joy and making positive changes. We'll talk about how changing our thoughts and actions can have a big impact on our overall happiness and fulfillment. The goal is to find our light and embrace the positive changes that await us.

Chapter 6:

Embracing Joy—Discovering Your Light and Committing to Positive Change

We frequently find ourselves overwhelmed and without a sense of wholeness after enduring an abusive relationship. After giving so much of ourselves to another person and allowing that relationship to consume us, we might feel empty and struggle to recall our true selves. Even if we choose to leave an unhealthy and unsafe situation, the aftermath can still evoke feelings of loss due to the significant time and emotional investment we made in it, as well as hopes that we had for a better future, even if the odds were stacked against us.

Once we establish clear boundaries and reclaim our space for healing, we can finally begin the journey of rediscovering our identity. At this point, we give ourselves permission to explore what brings us joy and fulfillment. This may be difficult at first because of the disconnect you feel with yourself. But don't let this discourage you. It all comes down to taking one step at a time.

As we gradually distance ourselves from toxic dynamics and reclaim our autonomy, we can embark on a journey of self-discovery and self-empowerment. We can gradually restore our sense of identity and find a fresh sense of purpose and fulfillment by practicing self-care and partaking in activities that speak to our true selves. It may take time and effort, but the path to self-discovery and personal growth is within our reach.

Take Care of Your Body and Mind

After leaving an abusive relationship, one can begin the healing process, which can be a challenging but empowering journey. As we prioritize self-care and rediscover our identities, we must nourish our bodies and minds with compassion and inclusivity. By taking the time to focus on our needs and our happiness, we can embark on a transformative healing process that promotes resilience and opens doors to a brighter future:

- **Embrace your emotions:** Allow yourself to feel and recognize emotions like anger, guilt, and sadness. Spend some time with these unpleasant feelings to realize your strength in facing them. Befriending your negative emotions will aid you in regaining control.

- **Find an outlet for your emotions:** Avoid keeping your feelings bottled up. Express them through journaling, listening, playing, or dancing to music that resonates with your emotions or any other creative outlets to release and process your emotions.

- **Work with a therapist:** Seek professional help by working with a therapist experienced in trauma and abuse. Therapy can provide valuable support, guidance, and tools to aid in your healing journey.

- **Prioritize self-care:** Make sure you eat well and on time and that you provide your body with all of the nutrients it requires. Sleep can affect both our physical and mental well-being. As a result, it's critical to prioritize getting enough sleep on a consistent basis. Maintaining your health is essential for your overall well-being and recovery.

- **Be patient and kind to yourself:** Forgive yourself for any perceived mistakes or shortcomings. Remember that you didn't choose to be exploited, and leaving the relationship was a courageous decision. Avoid self-blame and focus on rebuilding your self-worth and self-esteem.

- **Practice gratitude:** Practice gratitude by consciously acknowledging and appreciating the positive aspects of your life. Even little things like sunlight, ice cream, and great music can go on your list of things to be grateful for. This can help shift your focus towards the present and promote a sense of well-being.

Allow yourself to heal and grow by being gentle with yourself. Accept the power of self-care, seek help from understanding individuals or professionals, and never underestimate your own strength.

Let Nature In

Allowing nature into your life can be a life-changing and rejuvenating experience. Accept the natural world's beauty and reap its many benefits. Here are a few ideas to get you started:

- Take leisurely walks through a forest or park, soaking in the sounds of rustling leaves and the scent of fresh air. Listen to the sound of birds chirping or the wind whistling. This type of connection with nature can promote relaxation and inner peace.

- Take a stroll along the beach and listen to the sound of the waves crashing in time with you while feeling the sand between your toes. The vastness of the ocean can provide perspective and a sense of awe, while its calming ambiance creates a tranquil state of mind.

- Explore the mountains and go on rejuvenating hikes. As you climb, take in the refreshing mountain air and marvel at the stunning views. The combination of physical exercise and the natural beauty of the surroundings can be stimulating and inspiring.

- Sail on a lake, river, or even the ocean to explore waterways by boat. You may experience a sense of tranquility and relaxation as a result of the boat's gentle rocking and peaceful water views.

- Observe the mesmerizing colors of a sunset or sunrise. Find a peaceful area and take a moment to reflect while taking in the mesmerizing colors and the serene change from day to night. These mind-blowing experiences can make you feel restored and grateful.

You might also find other ways to incorporate nature into your life, such as gardening, birdwatching, or just finding a quiet place to sit and take in your surroundings. Remember that nature has a way of bringing us back to earth, calming our souls, and serving as a constant reminder of our own resilience and beauty.

Connect With Animals

On your journey, establishing a connection with animals can bring you great joy and healing. Our wounds can be soothed by their unwavering love, compassionate presence, and pure companionship. Animals have a special way of touching our hearts, providing comfort, and reassuring us that there are still good and kind people in the world. These kinds of creatures have the capacity to reflect our feelings, offer consolation, and aid us in rediscovering the beauty of unrequited love. To strengthen our bonds with our furry friends, consider trying out the below ideas:

- **Foster or adopt an animal:** Giving a furry friend a home and a place in your heart can bring countless amounts of love and companionship. To experience the joy of nurturing and being nurtured in return, think about taking a pet under your wing.

- **Visit a zoo or petting farm:** It can be fun and instructive to interact with animals at a zoo or petting farm. Interacting with a variety of species can foster a sense of wonder, appreciation for nature, and a stronger connection to the animal kingdom.

- **Walk a dog:** Offering to walk dogs from local shelters or helping neighbors in need leads to a win-win situation. You'll not only get some exercise and fresh air, but you'll also be providing much-needed companionship to these adorable creatures.

- **Volunteer at an animal shelter:** Giving your time and skills to an animal shelter is a meaningful way to help. Volunteering allows you to connect with animals while also supporting a worthy cause, whether it's providing care, socializing with animals, or assisting with administrative tasks.

- **Attending a dog show:** This can be an exciting experience where you can see the incredible skills, beauty, and bond that dogs and their handlers have. It's an opportunity to recognize the incredible bond that exists between humans and animals.

Always remember to treat animals with respect and kindness. Every interaction has the potential to improve your well-being while also strengthening the bond between humans and animals.

Take Pleasure in Routine Activities

Finding solace and joy in routine activities after leaving an abusive relationship can be a powerful source of healing and self-care. Familiar rituals and new experiences can provide a sense of comfort, stability, and renewal, paving the way for a journey of self-discovery and happiness.

- Begin your day with a cup of your favorite morning beverage, whether it's a soothing cup of coffee, tea, or any other soothing beverage. Allow yourself a moment of peace to savor the flavors and enjoy the morning silence.

- Relax by treating yourself to a rejuvenating soak in a hot tub or bath, accompanied by your favorite beverage. Allow the warm water to wash away any stress or tension, creating a peaceful haven for reflection and relaxation.

- Morning journaling after waking up can be a therapeutic practice for expressing your thoughts, feelings, and goals. Make time to write down your thoughts, dreams, and gratitude, allowing for self-reflection and personal growth.

- Try listening to podcasts that interest you to engage your mind and expand your knowledge. Podcasts can provide valuable insights, inspiration, and entertainment, whether it's a topic you're interested in or an avenue for exploration.

- Make a special dinner for yourself or gather your friends for a delicious meal. Prepare a meal that will nourish your body and soul, and relish the experience of good food and company. It's an opportunity to make lasting memories and strengthen bonds.

- Read books that capture your imagination to immerse yourself in the world of literature. Consider joining a book club to participate in lively discussions, meet other book lovers, and broaden your literary horizons.

Remember, these are just a few ideas for incorporating joy into your daily routine. Explore activities that speak to you and give yourself time to enjoy the simple pleasures of life.

Step Outside

Getting out of the house and exploring the world becomes an important part of rediscovering yourself after leaving an abusive relationship. Here are some ideas for embracing new experiences and feeding your soul:

- **Have a lunch date with a friend:** Take pleasure in a delicious meal while conversing and laughing heartily with a dependable friend.

- **Go out for a movie:** Allow yourself to be swept away to various worlds and feelings by losing yourself in the magic of storytelling on the big screen.

- **Visit a local museum or art show:** Indulge your senses in the splendor of art and culture to inspire and renew you.

- **Take a cooking class:** Discover the world of culinary delights by learning new recipes and techniques and connecting with others who have a similar interest in food.

- **Volunteer at a school or senior center:** Give back to your community by volunteering your time and skills, making meaningful connections, and making a difference in the lives of others.

- **Attend a concert:** As you immerse yourself in the energy of live performances, allow the music to uplift your spirit and ignite your emotions.

- **Go out dancing:** Embrace the joy of movement and connect with your body in a liberating and empowering way as you let go of your inhibitions on the dance floor.

Keep in mind that these ideas are only a starting point and that you should pay attention to your own desires and interests. Allow yourself the freedom to try new activities and experiences that spark your interest and foster a sense of self-discovery, joy, and personal growth.

Tackle a Project

Taking on projects can be a powerful way to regain control and make a fresh start. By working on worthwhile projects and seizing new opportunities, we can rebuild our lives with resiliency and forge an independent and fulfilling future.

- **Organize your living space:** Decluttering and organizing can provide a sense of calm and clarity. Begin by organizing common areas such as your closet, bedroom, kitchen, and garage.

- **Donate or sell unused items:** Allow yourself to let go of possessions that no longer serve you. Give them away or sell them to make room for new beginnings and assist those in need.

- **Start a hydroponic grow garden:** This can be a fulfilling and therapeutic activity. Plant cultivation can provide a sense of nurturing and growth while also reconnecting you with nature.

- **Decorate and update a room:** Transform an outdated or uninspiring space. Consider incorporating personal touches and decor that complement your new sense of self and style.

- **Consider a move if it's beneficial:** Consider whether a change in your living situation, whether for financial or emotional reasons, could aid in your healing and growth. If it is within your financial means, moving can provide a new beginning and a sense of empowerment.

- **Learn new skills:** Take a class or look into online learning platforms to learn new skills or hone existing ones. Learning can boost confidence and open the door to new opportunities.

- **Explore various revenue streams:** Consider diversifying your income streams by freelancing, starting a side business, or investing in ventures that align with your interests and passions.

The emphasis is on self-discovery and living a meaningful life. Choose projects and activities that are meaningful to you and bring you joy, allowing yourself the freedom to experiment with and embrace new possibilities.

Art

Art can be a very powerful and therapeutic way to rediscover yourself. You can tap into your inner creativity and find solace, healing, and a sense of empowerment through artistic expression. Finding creative outlets allows you to express yourself, tell your story, and make something beautiful and meaningful. Art can be a transformative tool for self-discovery and self-expression, whether it's shaping clay, capturing moments with a camera, or immersing yourself in the colors of paint. Don't be afraid to try new things, and let your artistic journey serve as a catalyst for personal growth and healing. Below are a few of the many ways in which you can tap into your artistic bone to reconnect with yourself.

- **Pottery:** Make beautiful creations out of clay by getting your hands messy and allowing the tactile experience to serve as a therapeutic outlet.

- **Painting:** Express yourself by using colors and brushstrokes that let your emotions spill out onto the canvas and produce art that is distinctly you.

- **Scrapbooking:** Create a visual narrative that highlights your journey and achievements by gathering and placing special photos, mementos, and words in a meaningful and visually pleasing way.

- **Jewelry Making:** Craft personalized pieces that reflect your personality and story while transforming materials into wearable art with special meaning.

- **Crocheting or knitting:** Allow your hands to weave threads of comfort and warmth as you engage in the rhythmic and soothing process of creating fabrics and clothes.

- **Needlepoint:** Immerse yourself in the meditative act of stitching intricate designs, and find peace and mindfulness in the precision and repetition of each stitch.

- **Quilting:** Make a quilt out of fabric scraps to represent your resilience and the beautiful patchwork of your life.

- **Photography:** Capture the world through your lens, focusing on the beauty in your surroundings and discovering new perspectives that will inspire and uplift your spirit.

Remember that art is a personal journey with no right or wrong ways to express yourself creatively. Allow yourself the freedom to experiment with various mediums and discover what resonates with you. Allow art to be a transformative tool for your healing, self-discovery, and celebration of your unique journey.

Fitness

Physical activity not only helps us rebuild our physical strength, but it also improves our self-esteem by instilling a sense of accomplishment and pride in who we are becoming. Physical activity revitalizes us, giving us the energy and resilience to tackle any obstacles that may arise during the day.

- **Golf:** Begin a tranquil journey through the greens, taking in the fresh air and peaceful surroundings while honing your skills and focusing on self-improvement.

- **Yoga:** Find recuperation through the practice of yoga, which combines physical postures, breathing exercises, and mindfulness to promote inner strength, flexibility, and peace of mind.

- **Pilates:** With the help of Pilates' precise movements and controlled breathing techniques, you can strengthen your core, increase your flexibility, and foster body awareness.

- **Water Aerobics:** Immerse yourself in the exhilarating world of aerobics. Enjoy a soothing soak in the water and enjoy low-impact exercises that improve cardiovascular fitness and joint flexibility.

- **Weight or Strength Training:** Incorporate weight or strength training into your routine to increase physical strength, boost confidence, and improve body composition, with the goal of empowering yourself through progress and personal achievements.

- **Kayaking:** Discover the freedom and tranquility of kayaking while immersing yourself in nature and getting a full-body workout that strengthens your muscles and lifts your spirits.

- **Cross-Country or Downhill Skiing:** Enjoy the exhilaration of gliding across snow-covered terrain while reaping the benefits of cardiovascular exercise by embracing the beauty of winter landscapes through cross-country or downhill skiing.

- **Biking:** Enjoy the independence and feeling of adventure that riding provides, whether on trails or highways, while boosting cardiovascular fitness and leg strength.

- **Spin Class:** Participate in a high-energy spin class where positive music and inspiring instructors force you ahead, testing your boundaries and instilling a sense of success.

- **Swimming:** Dive into a refreshing pool and enjoy the relaxing and revitalizing effects of swimming. Enjoy a full-body exercise while also benefiting from the calming qualities of water.

- **Dance Classes:** Join lessons in salsa, ballet, hip-hop, movement therapy, or any other form of dance that appeals to you. Explore the expressive world of dance, which will not only increase physical fitness but also self-expression, confidence, and connection with your body.

We may tap into our inner power, build a good body image, and foster a sense of general well-being by partaking in these activities or discovering new types of physical activity that resonate with us. Remember that each person's road to self-discovery and recovery is unique, so select activities that bring you joy and make you feel alive.

Spiritual

Being spiritual signifies a connection to something higher than ourselves as well as a search for meaning, purpose, and inner serenity. Spiritual practices nourish our mental and physical well-being and provide consolation and guidance as we travel the path of recovery. We may find strength, clarity, and a renewed sense of hope by connecting with our faith, fostering holistic healing, and empowering us to reclaim our genuine selves.

- **Deep breathing:** Take breaks throughout the day to practice deep, deliberate breathing. This easy meditation can enable you to calm yourself, alleviate stress, and gain mental clarity.

- **Meditation:** Make time for meditation and allow yourself to be totally present and aware of the current moment. You can begin as a novice by following guided meditations. Even 5–10 minutes each day can make an immense impact. Meditation can help you relax, reflect, and connect with your inner self more deeply.

- **Affirmations:** Use affirmations that are consistent with your spiritual principles. Repeat to yourself positive and encouraging affirmations to reinforce your self-worth, resilience, and ability to rebuild your life.

- **Being present:** Focus on this particular moment in time to cultivate awareness. Allow yourself to fully experience and appreciate the present moment, letting go of past traumas and future concerns.

- **Meet with like-minded people:** Seek out and connect with others who hold similar spiritual ideas to you. Participating in conversations and activities with individuals who share similar interests may create a sense of belonging, support, and understanding.

- **Create a sense of support and community:** Create a network of people who will encourage and inspire you on your spiritual path. Surround yourself with individuals who will support, guide, and provide a safe environment for expression.

- **Read spiritual literature:** Find books and literature that represent your spiritual views. Dive into the knowledge, lessons, and experiences of others to obtain insights and perspectives on your own path.

Spiritual practices are incredibly personal, and it is critical to figure out what connects with you individually. Allow yourself the opportunity to explore and find pursuits that nourish your soul while encouraging self-discovery, healing, and a stronger connection to your spiritual journey.

Exercise

Creating a Pleasure and Gratitude Calendar

1. Think for a moment about the things you enjoy doing and the things that make you happy. Think about your true passions and what you can devote time to.

2. Put the next four weeks on a calendar and schedule precise time periods for those activities. Begin by committing to implementing these on at least one day every week, even if just for a short time. Increase it progressively to 2–3 days per week if possible.

3. As you participate in these activities, have a positive mentality, consciously turning from negativity to positivity. Even when negative or self-defeating ideas come, don't berate yourself for them. Simply acknowledge them and shift your focus to the joy and contentment these hobbies provide you.

4. Avoid things that you feel forced to undertake but do not enjoy. The idea is to make room and time for things that actually offer you joy and to which you are willing to commit.

5. After 31 days, reflect on your experience with the activities and schedule. Consider the following questions:

    Did I follow through on the commitments I made?

    Did I have enough time to really immerse myself in those activities?

What were the activities that I truly enjoyed?

Did I have enough time for the activities, or did they seem rushed and routine?

Nurturing Support

1. Recognize the value of a support system that includes a therapist. If you haven't already, plan regular meetings with a therapist to provide continuing support and direction.

2. Make a list of a few people in your life to whom you may turn for nurturing and support. Consider friends, family members, or trustworthy individuals who have demonstrated compassion and understanding.

3. Reach out to those people and see if you can arrange a meeting or two throughout the month to participate in things that you both like. It may be getting together for a drink or coffee, doing some physical exercise together, or doing anything else equally pleasurable.

4. Engage in these meetups and immerse yourself in the experience. Take notice of how they make you feel and how they encourage you.

5. Reflect on these encounters at the conclusion of the month and analyze their influence on your well-being and sense of support.

Gratitude Reflection

1. Consider and appreciate the positive experiences, people, and things in your life.

2. Make a comprehensive list, thanking and expressing gratitude for the blessings you now have. Concentrate on elements that offer you joy, contentment, and feelings of gratitude.

3. Review your list and take in the rewarding feelings that come from recognizing and appreciating what you have in your life right now.

It's important to acknowledge the importance of taking stock of what gives us joy and calm. We can rediscover the light within ourselves by reflecting on the things that used to bring us joy and exploring new experiences. Furthermore, cultivating positive connections and prioritizing self-care for our minds and bodies contribute to our overall well-being.

Challenges will inevitably occur along the road. The following chapter will go over valuable techniques for constructing a safety net to help you handle setbacks and continue on your path to recovery and self-discovery. We'll look at ways to psychologically prepare for setbacks and understand the significance of treating ourselves with kindness when they occur. Remember that failures do not define us. They are opportunities for growth, and we can confront them with power and resolve if we cultivate self-love and resilience.

Chapter 7:

Navigating Setbacks—Building a Foundation of Self-Love and Resilience

Once we leave an abusive relationship, it's important to take certain steps to heal and recover. Understanding and sitting with our emotions, setting boundaries, and finding joy and fulfillment in our lives again are all essential parts of this process. While we have already delved into these steps in detail, it is crucial to emphasize their significance once more. They serve as catalysts for healing, guiding us along the road to recovery.

However, it's important to recognize that any process of growth and healing is not linear. Setbacks are inevitable, and each setback brings with it a new lesson, sometimes even more impactful than before. These obstacles can be frustrating, particularly when they arise after a period of gratifying progress and healing. Nevertheless, it's crucial to remember that setbacks are a natural part of the healing process. During these challenging circumstances, it's essential to be gentle, kind, and compassionate towards ourselves. Do not blame or punish yourself for encountering these roadblocks. Give yourself the grace to be human and allow your emotions to rise and fall like the tide.

With each setback, we discover newfound strength and resilience, equipping us with the tools to face future challenges. Over time, we may even notice these setbacks occurring less frequently as we continue to grow.

As you read on, you will explore the typical kinds of setbacks you might encounter or expect to face. You will also be provided with various tools and approaches that can assist you in facing and overcoming these challenges. By embracing these strategies, you will continue progressing on your road to recovery and ultimately find healing and growth.

Common Setbacks

The journey of an abuse victim does not end with leaving an abusive relationship; it is merely the initial step in their path towards healing from a trauma bond. Individuals who have experienced abuse in relationships often endure relationship trauma, leading to intense emotions such as rage, anger, cognitive difficulties, and the re-experiencing of traumatic events. These upsetting thoughts and sentiments about their abusive ex might last for a long time after the relationship has ended, affecting both their psychological and bodily well-being.

Setbacks are a universal experience, and recovering from abuse, particularly when it has been traumatic, significantly heightens our vulnerability. In such moments, having a well-prepared plan in place becomes crucial, along with trusting that our emotions will gradually ease with time and nurturing. It is vital not to suppress these feelings and pretend they don't exist, as doing so only prolongs the pain and hinders the recovery process. This is when our resilience is tested the most, and it may require spending more time alone as it consumes a greater amount of our mental and physical energy.

However, it is imperative to have faith that this phase will pass, and we will emerge stronger on the other side:

- **Flashbacks**: These are intense and intrusive thoughts that recall a traumatic incident. They may be incredibly disturbing, making a person feel as if they are reliving these unwelcome experiences over and over again.

- **Fear or distress**: Those who have ended an abusive relationship may experience intense emotions like anger, fear, stress, or anxiety when entering new relationships or encountering situations that trigger their traumatic experiences. This might result in avoiding the causes, activities, or people who elicit these negative emotions.

- **Sadness**: Abuse survivors frequently experience uncontrollable crying and, contrastingly, feelings of numbness. They may suffer from severe grief and find it difficult to completely experience emotions.

- **Guilt and shame**: Self-blame and self-loathing may cause you to alienate yourself from others and make it difficult to maintain relationships with them.

- **Insomnia and nightmares**: Sleep habits can be disrupted by relationship trauma, making it harder to fall or remain asleep. Nightmares associated with stressful events might further disrupt undisturbed sleep.

- **Trust issues**: Experiencing emotional, physical, or sexual boundary violations in an abusive relationship can cause a person to become more skeptical and distrustful of themselves and others. Survivors may become hypervigilant about their environment and social interactions.

- **Frustration**: Survivors may become frustrated because they believe they are not making progress or that things are not improving as rapidly as they would like.

- **Overwhelming anger or rage:** Unresolved sorrow and unprocessed emotions can show as rage or severe anger, signaling the need for more healing and processing.

- **Missing your ex:** Despite the violent nature of the relationship, survivors may miss their ex-partner owing to the complicated emotions and attachment dynamics involved.

- **Euphoric recall:** This entails selectively recalling happy memories and losing oneself in romanticized fantasies, nostalgic adventures, and passionate intimacy. It's like being drawn back to the burning house from which you fled. Because abusive relationships are addictive, euphoric recall can be dangerous, leading to relapse.

- **Feeling that nobody gets it:** Survivors may feel isolated and misunderstood by those around them who have not been subjected to similar abusive conditions.

- **Exaggerated emotional reactions:** Emotional responses may become intensified and overblown as a result of the trauma experienced in the abusive relationship.

- **Increased irritability:** Survivors may find themselves becoming more easily annoyed or agitated, probably as a result of persistent stress and emotional strain.

- **Loneliness or isolation:** After leaving an abusive relationship, survivors may experience feelings of loneliness or isolation because they have broken relationships with their prior support networks or feel detached from others.

- **Impulsive relationships:** As they traverse their recovery journey, some survivors may participate in impulsive relationships, seeking affirmation or attempting to fill the void left by the abusive relationship.

- **Sexual dysfunction:** The consequences of an abusive relationship can have an influence on survivors' sexual well-being, resulting in problems and obstacles in their sexual interactions.

- **Distrust in the world and life as you know it:** Distrust in the world and in life as you know it: Abuse may damage survivors' trust in the world and in life, making it difficult to reclaim a sense of safety and everyday life.

- **Feeling inadequate or unworthy:** Survivors may have emotions of inferiority or worthlessness, which are frequently the result of negative messages and devaluation received during the abusive relationship.

It's crucial to remember that these setbacks are common but not universal, and each person's healing process is unique. Seeking professional assistance and support from reputable folks can be extremely helpful in overcoming these obstacles.

How to Plan for Setbacks and Deal With Them

Reaching out for support and actively working through difficult emotions is a display of strength, self-love, and healing. It's never a sign of weakness; in fact, it's quite the opposite. By taking these steps, we demonstrate our commitment to protecting the inner child within us and prioritizing her well-being above all else.

1. **Validate your emotions:** Accepting and acknowledging the emotions that come following setbacks is critical. Allow yourself to experience and process your emotions, whether they be anger, sadness, fear, or a combination of these. Recognize that these feelings are a natural reaction to the trauma you've experienced.

2. **Take time for reflection:** Setbacks allow you to pause and reflect on your road to recovery. Use this time to analyze your progress, revisit your goals, and discover any triggers or patterns that are impeding your healing. Consider what needs

to be prioritized and change your self-care practices accordingly.

3. **Learn and grow:** Every stumble provides an opportunity to pick up important lessons. Determine the particular triggers or conditions that contributed to the setback and consider how you may handle such situations differently in the future. Accept the setback as a chance for personal development and empowerment, and use the information acquired to enhance your resilience.

4. **Cultivate self-compassion:** As you face challenges in your recovery, be kind, compassionate, and forgiving to yourself. Challenge self-blame and negative self-talk to practice self-compassion. Remind yourself that setbacks are a natural part of the healing process and that you deserve to be patient and compassionate with yourself on this path.

5. **Seek support:** Reach out to a therapist or counselor who specializes in trauma, narcissistic abuse, PTSD, and recovery. They can provide guidance, validation, and coping strategies tailored to your specific needs. Consider support groups or online communities where you can connect with individuals who have similar experiences and share advice and encouragement.

6. **Celebrate progress:** Recognize and appreciate your triumphs thus far, especially in the face of hardships. Recognize that setbacks are not a sign of failure but rather opportunities to grow. Celebrate your tenacity and strength throughout the healing process.

7. **Stay mindful and grounded:** To be present and grounded amid setbacks, use mindfulness practices such as deep breathing, meditation, or grounding exercises. These techniques

can help you regulate your emotions, manage anxiety, and retain a sense of stability in the face of adversity.

Although setbacks in the process of recovering from abuse trauma can be difficult, it is critical to remember that these traumas do not define you or determine your value. While they may reappear from time to time, they are only part of your story, not the whole. You have the ability to influence how these events shape you and how you define yourself. As you continue on your recovery path, embrace your resilience, strength, and capacity for growth. You are defined not by your past but by the person you are becoming.

Exercise

When we have setbacks on our path to healing and recovery, having practical exercises and techniques in place to navigate and conquer the problems that occur can prove quite beneficial. We may equip ourselves to tackle problems with resilience and a sense of control by proactively engaging in these activities. When you have setbacks, try using the following example practices as tools to lead you toward healing and progress. Remember that each exercise may be customized to your own requirements and tastes, ensuring that you find the ways that work best for you.

Overwhelming Sadness

Acknowledge what you've experienced and that feeling sad and shedding tears is completely normal. Allow yourself to feel and process the emotions.

When I'm sad, my plan will be to:
- *Cry and release my emotions.*
- *Find comfort in talking to a supportive friend who can lend a listening ear.*
- *Take some time alone to reflect and work through my feelings.*

Frustration

Feeling frustrated and stuck is a common setback. Recognize that it's normal to feel this way.

When I'm frustrated, I will engage in activities that help restore my mental equilibrium, such as:

- *Deep breathing exercises*
- *Journaling my thoughts and frustrations*
- *Participating in physical activity or exercise*
- *Meditating*
- *Socializing with a friend*
- *Volunteering*
- *Finding a creative outlet*

Overwhelming Anger or Rage

Many times, overwhelming anger or rage indicate unresolved grief. Acknowledge your anger and allow yourself to feel its source. Utilize this opportunity for catharsis and release.

My plan will be to:

- *Journal about my anger and its underlying causes.*
- *Engage in physical activities that can help release pent-up energy, such as going for a run, hitting a punching bag, or practicing martial arts.*
- *Find a safe space to scream or express my anger in a controlled way.*
- *Write a letter to the source of the anger without sending it, using it as a means of catharsis.*

- *Write a letter to myself, offering self-compassion and understanding.*

Remember that these are only a few examples, and it's critical to identify coping mechanisms that work best for you. Feel free to modify and tweak these methods to meet your own requirements and tastes. Overcoming failures necessitates self-awareness, acceptance, and a willingness to experiment with diverse strategies for navigating and overcoming difficult emotions.

Setbacks are inevitable, and they can sometimes shake the very core of our being. However, by proactively implementing the exercises and strategies we've discussed, we may build strong safety nets that catch us when we fall and give us the power we need to get back up. You have made important efforts toward laying a firm foundation for facing setbacks with courage and grace by establishing safety nets and engaging in activities that promote self-compassion, emotional expression, and personal growth. These safety nets not only provide us with comfort and security, but they also act as reminders of our own resilience and ability for growth.

Looking ahead to the next chapter, you will begin the process of rewriting your story and charting your own course. It will be a transforming journey that will help you determine your existing principles, desires, and objectives. You will find yourself by rewiring the limiting ideas in your head and accepting the power of your own decisions. Through a variety of growth strategies, you will reinvent the meaning of your life on your terms.

Take that leap of faith to discover your incredible potential as you rebuild your narratives and strive to live your truth. Prepare to go into the depths of self-discovery and embrace the seemingly unlimited possibilities that await you.

Chapter 8:

Rewriting Your Narrative—

Defining

Your Own Path

There comes a point in someone's healing path when you have the opportunity to rebuild the foundation of your values, aspirations, and objectives. This stage is full of strength and empowerment, especially if you have undergone trauma or have recently ended a long-term unhealthy relationship. It's a period dedicated completely to your own self-discovery and advancement.

This phase invites you to completely focus on yourself, contemplate what you actually seek to accomplish, and identify the abilities you want to grow and expand on. It is an introspective time when you may fearlessly let go of everything that no longer fits who you are or who you want to be.

Take the time to consider and reflect on the principles that resonate with your soul, particularly in the many aspects of your life. Examine the areas where you want to improve personally and the abilities you want to nurture. Embrace this transformative stage, for it's a profound opportunity to rediscover your true self and pave the way toward a future that aligns with your deepest desires.

Your Values, Dreams, and Goals

When you reach this stage in your journey, you may explore previous ambitions and dreams, allowing you to develop a fresh and real version of yourself that has always existed within you. It is a stage in which you may focus on themes of identity and intimacy without being constrained by the limitations that trauma may have placed in the past. While your recovery may not be complete, you have acquired skills for self-care and navigating stressful circumstances, ensuring that your PTSD symptoms do not overwhelm you. As a result, you will most likely become more focused on the present, free of the weight of the past.

Now that you've established space for yourself, it's time to consider what you genuinely want out of life. Your values describe what you value in how you live and operate. They direct your priorities and act as indicators of whether your life is in line with your goals. When your life is out of sync with your basic beliefs, your body feels uncomfortable and uneasy, which leads to dissatisfaction. As a result, it is critical to carefully determine your values.

Knowing your values allows your profession, personal relationships, and hobbies to reflect what is genuinely important to you, resulting in a sense of contentment and improved mental health. When your profession is in line with your values, passion drives motivation, which leads to success. Personal values define your sense of purpose, impacting your personality, goal-setting, and life actions. You can accept your genuine self by making decisions that are consistent with your ideals.

Moreover, personal values play a vital role in relationships. Making your values known improves your relationships with friends and coworkers. It becomes easier to express your wants and emotions, preventing detrimental suppression. Understanding your values allows you to find and nurture relationships with like-minded people, forming meaningful and supportive bonds.

Adopting personal values improves self-awareness, which is essential for your own growth. Values keep you focused on your goals, interests, and constraints. They shed light on your career and personal goals. Without personal principles, determining what you want to achieve, or your full potential becomes difficult. The first step toward self-improvement is self-awareness, which allows you to advocate for yourself and make better decisions while also building relationships.

It's okay if you're still figuring out what beliefs and ideals are important to you. The process takes time, and you may have many or few personal values that you prioritize. The trick, though, is to ensure that you live by your values, enabling them to influence your decisions and actions, resulting in a more satisfying and authentic existence.

Your Character

It's essential to evaluate your personal core principles while contemplating the values that determine your character. These values describe the essential concepts and beliefs that govern and form your conduct and character:

- **Self-empowerment:** Recognizing your worth, setting boundaries, and restoring your own agency are all part of this process. This value motivates you to take charge of your life and make decisions that reflect your actual aspirations and ideals.

- **Courage**: Having courage allows you to face your fears, address previous trauma, and venture beyond your comfort zone. It involves mustering the strength to tell your truth, advocate for yourself, and to take the essential measures toward healing and recovery.

- **Integrity:** This value stresses honesty, sincerity, and living in accordance with one's underlying convictions. Embracing integrity entails being truthful to oneself and others, keeping oneself accountable for one's actions, and developing trust in one's relationships.

- **Resilience:** This principle recognizes the difficulties you have overcome and emphasizes your potential to recover, adapt, and grow stronger. In the face of hardship, it entails discovering inner strength, establishing coping methods, and adopting a growth mentality.

- **Personal growth and continuous learning:** These values highlight the significance of growing, learning, and striving for self-improvement. These principles motivate you to seek out new possibilities, push yourself, and adopt a growth mentality for the rest of your life.

By adopting and living these personal core values, you establish a moral compass in your character that drives your decisions and actions. They provide the foundation for a life of meaning, fulfillment, and authenticity. Your values influence how you interact with others, instilling kindness, responsibility, and perseverance in the face of hardship. They give you a feeling of purpose, helping you manage the complexity of life with integrity and compassion. As you consistently cultivate and cherish these values, they not only define your character but also serve as a source of strength and inspiration, enabling you to make a good influence and live a life that represents your innermost convictions.

Emotional

When it comes to the emotional aspects of your life, there are various values that may have a significant impact on your overall happiness and well-being. These principles serve as a guidepost for traversing your emotional terrain and cultivating a meaningful inner world. Consider the following emotional values:

- **Self-compassion:** Compassion for oneself and others is still an important trait because it fosters understanding, forgiveness, and empathy. Self-compassion is treating oneself with love, patience, and gentleness while also providing the same compassion to others who may have endured trauma.

- **Trust**: Another crucial characteristic is trust, both in oneself and in others, which allows for the repair of connections and the creation of a sense of security.

- **Boundaries**: This is important in terms of establishing and maintaining healthy limits and can empower individuals to prioritize their emotional well-being and protect themselves from further harm.

- **Honesty and authenticity:** These can contribute to the creation of a safe environment for emotional expression, enabling true relationships and self-discovery.

- **An optimistic outlook:** Embracing thankfulness and creating a positive mentality can help shift attention to the present and foster a sense of appreciation, supporting emotional well-being.

When you prioritize and incorporate these principles into your emotional journey, you open the door to a deeper awareness of yourself, encouraging resilience, compassion, and authenticity that may lead you to a life of greater emotional fulfillment and harmony.

Intellectual

Intellectual values are the concepts that govern your quest for knowledge, learning, and personal development. Adopting these beliefs empowers you to recover your intellectual liberty.

- **Critical thinking:** This becomes a significant intellectual asset, prompting you to question, analyze, and evaluate information, allowing you to make educated judgments and avoid deception.

- **Curiosity:** Cultivating curiosity develops a need for knowledge, inquiry, and a drive to comprehend the world around you. This is a crucial attribute to cultivate.

- **Open-mindedness:** Having an open mind permits you to be receptive to new perspectives, ideas, and experiences, which promotes intellectual flexibility and personal growth.

- **Knowledge:** Empowering oneself with information and education is another important virtue since it allows you to broaden your horizons, learn new skills, and lay the groundwork for personal and professional success.

- **Creativity:** This is yet another important intellectual trait that pushes you to express yourself, seek new pathways of self-expression, and capitalize on your particular strengths and capabilities.

These principles lay the groundwork for broadening your intellectual horizons, discovering your particular strengths, and finding delight in the process of self-discovery and lifelong learning. Consider and embrace these intellectual ideals as you traverse your route to healing to restore a sense of intellectual strength, drive personal growth, and unleash new possibilities for a brighter future.

Life's Purpose

Finding meaning and purpose in life is a powerful and transformational journey, particularly for those who have experienced terrible trauma. The purpose is a guiding light that influences our actions, shapes our ambitions, and provides a feeling of direction and fulfillment. It may appear in many aspects of our lives, including work, relationships, spirituality, and personal growth. We begin to uncover the unique route that fits with our actual selves as we engage on the journey to discover our life's purpose, recognizing that meaning is fluid and may develop in response to our shifting priorities and life experiences.

Pursuing your life's purpose is a very personal and introspective undertaking formed by your own healing and self-discovery journey. It is critical to acknowledge that your purpose may differ from others, reflecting the uniqueness of your experiences and goals. It's natural for questions to emerge when you consider your life purpose.

Who am I at my core when the pain and trauma have been separated?

Where do I fit in, surrounded by a welcoming community that fosters my development?

When do I feel truly fulfilled, having experiences that align with my deepest desires?

These questions invite you to delve into the depths of your being, reconnect with your authentic self, and forge a path that is meaningful and joyful.

Embrace the fact that your purpose is unique and ever-changing and that it will develop alongside your personal progress. Accept the questions that come as signposts on the journey to self-discovery. You may create a life filled with purpose and meaning by discovering your real identity, discovering your feeling of belonging, and enjoying the moments that offer fulfillment. Remember that your mission is a lifelong adventure—an ongoing discovery of your potential and the significant influence you can have on the world around you.

Family

Exploring and reevaluating your family values while recovering from abuse trauma may be a hard and emotionally fraught process. Because the notion of family may evoke both terrible memories and beloved experiences, it is critical to approach this exploration with caution and self-compassion.

Reflecting on your family values entails thinking about what you actually want in your relationships, the limits you need to set for your own well-being, and the sort of support and connection you deserve. This insight can assist you in redefining your concept of family, understanding that it extends beyond biological connections to include chosen relationships that elevate and nourish your recovery path. You can lay the groundwork for good and nurturing interactions in your life by purposefully fostering values like trust, respect, healthy communication, and mutual support.

While rebuilding and redefining your familial ties may take time and work, the process allows you to craft a new narrative that values your well-being, safety, and emotional growth. Finally, by connecting your family values with your own healing and growth, you may prepare the road for more rewarding and supportive relationships that extend beyond traditional conceptions of family.

Social

When evaluating values related to your social life, it is critical to create a healthy, empowered social environment that promotes your well-being. It is important to surround oneself with people who respect your boundaries, ideals, and growth. Prioritizing connections that promote optimism, understanding, and support offers a safe environment for you to be yourself. Connecting with individuals who uplift and encourage you can help you restore trust and reclaim your sense of belonging. Creating such an atmosphere promotes healing, fosters resilience, and improves general well-being:

- **Connection:** It's important to embrace the value of connection because it promotes the development of sincere bonds with reliable people who uphold your boundaries and promote your growth.

- **Trustworthiness:** Being trustworthy is vital in both picking companions and establishing self-trust, allowing you to set appropriate boundaries and feel safe in social interactions.

- **Compassion:** This is an important value because it fosters empathy, compassion, and kindness toward oneself and others, consequently establishing a safe environment for healing and growth.

- **Boundaries and self-care:** These are important values to prioritize because they allow you to set boundaries, convey your requirements, and prioritize your emotional well-being.

- **Reciprocity:** The principle of reciprocity emphasizes healthy, mutually beneficial relationships in which support, respect, and care are given and received.

By incorporating these principles into your social interactions, you may build a supportive and empowering network that supports healing, development, and a restored feeling of belonging. Remember that your path to re-establishing your social life is unique, and by being loyal to your principles, you may form relationships that contribute to your overall well-being and help you move forward with confidence and resilience.

Health and Fitness

Taking care of your physical health may have a significant influence on your overall rehabilitation, allowing you to reclaim control, enhance your self-esteem, and improve your overall quality of life. Considering health and fitness principles may provide a guiding framework for making decisions that promote your well-being while navigating potential social barriers.

- **Self-care:** This entails paying attention to your body's demands and taking actions to improve your physical health. This value urges you to emphasize activities that promote self-nourishment, such as regular exercise, enough relaxation, and a well-balanced diet. Self-care not only improves your physical well-being but also fosters a sense of self-worth and self-love.

- **Balance:** When it comes to health and fitness, this means understanding the value of moderation and avoiding extremes. Striving for a balanced approach enables you to develop long-term habits that enhance well-being while avoiding self-judgment or preoccupation. It entails striking a good balance between exercise, diet, relaxation, and other parts of your life, thereby cultivating a harmonious relationship between your body and mind.

- **Self-discipline and self-compassion:** A good equilibrium of these principles is important in navigating situations involving health and fitness. This includes acknowledging that loving yourself means respecting yourself enough to continue showing up for yourself while also noting that everyone's journey is unique and that setbacks or deviations from a routine are natural. When faced with problems or perceived demands, self-compassion urges you to be kind to yourself. It entails practicing self-forgiveness, reframing negative self-talk, and accepting the concept of growth as a progressive and non-linear process.

Embracing health and fitness ideals can be transformative in terms of recovering your physical well-being and cultivating a good relationship with your body. As a result, you can confidently and gracefully deal with situations involving health and fitness. Adopting these ideals will not only benefit your physical health but will also improve your total well-being, allowing you to develop a sustainable and rewarding lifestyle that fosters recovery and personal growth.

Finances

As you discovered in Chapter 5, thinking about and accepting certain financial ideals can provide a sense of security, freedom, and empowerment. Financial responsibility becomes a critical virtue, requiring careful planning, spending tracking, and making sound financial judgments. Having an ideal of self-sufficiency motivates you to achieve financial independence, allowing you to rely on yourself and build a sense of security.

Prioritizing financial literacy allows you to comprehend topics like investing, savings, and debt management, allowing you to make wise financial decisions. Furthermore, cultivating a generous value helps you establish a healthy relationship with money, find satisfaction in giving resources, and support organizations that correspond with your beliefs. By adopting these financial ideals, you may reclaim control of your financial well-being, overcome any previous financial abuse, and lay the groundwork for a happier and more prosperous future.

Career

Navigating the world of professional options and goals may be an important part of your recovery process. Consider beliefs that connect with your career as you rebuild your life and regain your sense of self. This may play a critical role in building a work environment that supports development, fulfillment, and empowerment. You may build a career path that honors your needs, values, and general well-being by recognizing and embracing these principles.

When considering career values, it is critical to emphasize values that encourage self-care, honesty, and a sense of purpose:

- **Autonomy:** This is an important value to consider since it allows you to have control over your job, make independent choices, and set appropriate boundaries.

- **Respect:** A respectful work environment ensures that your worth, contributions, and personal boundaries are valued and respected. Creating a sense of safety and trust in the workplace becomes critical, allowing you to feel comfortable sharing your thoughts, problems, and demands.

- **Collaboration and teamwork:** These are also important values because they create healthy social connections and support networks. You can build professional relationships based on trust, respect, and shared goals by encouraging a feeling of cooperation.

- **Alignment:** Pursuing employment that corresponds to your particular ideals and interests can provide a greater sense of fulfillment and meaning. When your profession mirrors your values, you might discover more purpose and happiness in your job.

The consideration of career values allows you to choose a professional route that corresponds to your requirements, values, and general well-being. Keep in mind that your employment choices should empower and elevate you, as well as provide a secure and supportive atmosphere in which you may succeed. You may go on a professional journey that not only helps your recovery process but also allows you to construct a satisfying and rewarding future by honoring your work ideals.

Personal Space

Personal space refers to the limits and autonomy that we construct for ourselves in social interactions and relationships. It is critical for people on this path to evaluate values that promote self-respect, empowerment, and emotional well-being:

- **Boundaries:** Setting healthy boundaries becomes an important value because it allows you to clearly identify and explain your limitations and requirements, developing self-respect and preserving your well-being.

- **Respect:** Having respect for personal boundaries is equally important, highlighting the necessity of respecting others' space and consent, establishing trust, and supporting healthy relationships.

- **Trust:** Having trust in both yourself and others is essential for creating a sense of safety and security in your own space, allowing you to form deeper relationships and navigate social situations with confidence.

- **Authenticity:** Embracing authenticity helps you be true to yourself and state your needs without fear of being judged or compromising, building real interactions based on mutual respect and understanding.

By contemplating and nurturing these personal space ideals, you may promote a sense of empowerment, self-care, and emotional balance, allowing you to handle social situations with confidence and build relationships based on mutual respect and trust. Embracing these principles will help you regain your personal space, express your autonomy, and form healthy connections with others as you go through the recovery process.

Spirituality

Exploring spirituality throughout the recovery process from abuse trauma may be a tremendous source of peace, strength, and healing. Spirituality transcends religious connections and links us to something more than ourselves, offering a feeling of purpose, inner serenity, and connection to a higher power or universe.

In the midst of social barriers, embracing spiritual principles can serve as a guiding light for people negotiating the intricacies of recovering from abuse trauma:

- **Forgiveness:** This may be a critical spiritual virtue, not only towards others who have inflicted damage but also towards yourself. It entails releasing the burden of holding anger and embarking on a path of healing and release.

- **Self-love:** This is a necessity. It is critical to acknowledge your natural value and cultivate a profound feeling of compassion and love for oneself. This value gives you the ability to prioritize self-care, establish boundaries, and create a supportive relationship with your inner self.

- **Purpose:** Finding meaning and purpose is a vital spiritual value because it inspires you to explore your unique path, uncover your abilities, and contribute to the world in a way that is consistent with your innermost values and beliefs.

- **Gratitude:** Embracing gratitude as a spiritual value helps you find consolation and appreciation for the blessings that surround you, big or small, turning your emphasis to the positive aspects of life and cultivating a sense of abundance and resilience.

- **Community:** Seeking connection with a welcoming spiritual community or like-minded folks who share your ideals may help you navigate the hurdles of modern life and develop a sense of community and support.

Adopting spiritual principles can serve as a great tool for finding consolation, inner strength, and resilience as you continue on the road of healing from abuse trauma. These values provide a guiding framework for navigating life's challenges and cultivating a profound feeling of connection to something more than oneself. You can uncover a source of comfort, healing, and change by exploring and integrating spiritual principles, allowing you to regain your power and find renewed hope on your journey to recovery.

Setting the Groundwork to Support Your Growth

Following a journey of healing and growth after abuse trauma necessitates a deliberate and considered approach. It's an opportunity to establish systems that will foster your personal growth, enhance your sense of self, and set you on a constructive path for the future. You can open up a universe of transformational approaches that promote your growth and well-being by adopting a creative attitude and embracing an abundance of possibilities.

Adopting a growth mindset will serve as a foundation for your transformational journey as you pursue development and healing. It encompasses maintaining the conviction that your talents and intelligence can be developed through hard work and devotion, allowing you to view obstacles as chances for learning and progress. Educating oneself becomes a great instrument for personal development when combined with a growth mindset. It entails pursuing information, broadening your awareness of trauma, healing, and life as a whole, and arming yourself with the skills you'll need to walk your path to resilience and empowerment.

It's important to recognize that societal views and our own conditioned beliefs, which are often influenced by personal experiences, can operate as barriers to completely embracing life. Recognizing the power of these notions is critical since our attitude impacts our strength and capability. As a result, overcoming negative thinking patterns that impede growth requires reframing limiting beliefs and cognitive distortions. By purposefully challenging and shifting our perspective, we can adopt a confident and upbeat mindset that opens doors to personal advancement and fulfillment.

However, we must acknowledge that we cannot face all obstacles alone. Some personal challenges may feel overwhelming and confusing, making it difficult to navigate them on our own. Seeking the help of a therapist can prove particularly helpful at such times. Working with a therapist provides us with a caring and objective viewpoint on our recovery process. It provides a secure environment to process one's emotions, obtain useful insights, and build efficient coping methods. Through this therapeutic relationship, we can obtain the necessary guidance and tools to negotiate the intricacies of our experiences.

Furthermore, it is critical to fully engage in life and widen our horizons, particularly when it comes to volunteering for causes that kindle our enthusiasm. Engaging in such activities helps us channel our energy toward making a positive difference while interacting with like-minded others who share our ideals. Furthermore, forming a caring group around us reinforces our sense of belonging and gives much-needed encouragement as we traverse our healing journey.

Equally important is shifting our emphasis to the present moment and developing an abundant outlook on the future. Embracing the possibilities that await us opens the door to a new world of optimism, development, and renewed purpose. By intentionally adopting life choices that promote personal growth, we create a loving and transforming environment that supports our development, enhances our resilience, and paves the way for a future filled with healing, self-discovery, and deep personal empowerment.

Connect to Your Inner Child

Our inner child represents the essence of who we were before life's challenges and traumas impacted us. By nurturing and reconnecting with our inner child, we may tap into a wellspring of authenticity, joy, and resilience that can guide us toward healing and self-discovery.

To understand who we are and why we act the way we do, we must first understand our own story and have the courage to explore our past. Early childhood traumas frequently impact how we identify and protect ourselves, influencing our behavior in ways we may not be completely aware of. By confronting the memories and traumas that surface, we receive essential insights into our behavior patterns and coping processes.

Recognizing that the coping mechanisms we established as children were means of survival at the time, we may now offer compassion to that child within us. We can assure ourselves that we are no longer the defenseless kids we once were and that the adult within us is here to protect our inner child. By recognizing and processing these triggers and emotions, we can deliberately choose to let go of defensive mechanisms that no longer serve us and handle life's obstacles in a more logical, healthy, and beneficial manner.

Another crucial part of reconnecting with our inner child is creating a secure and supportive environment for exploration and expression. Engage in activities that elicit a sense of fun and wonder, enabling yourself to let go of adult duties and commitments for a short time. This could involve indulging in creative pursuits, exploring nature, or doing things that offer you joy and a sense of freedom.

When we develop a strong connection with our inner child, we might notice an increase in our daily creativity, spontaneity, and sincerity. This link becomes a guiding force, assisting us in making decisions that are in line with our genuine aspirations and beliefs.

Remember that reconnecting with your inner child does not imply regressing or denying maturity but rather embracing the joyful, carefree, and imaginative attributes of yourself. We encourage our personal progress and pave the road for a more satisfying and joyous existence by blending the wisdom and resilience we've learned as adults with the pure, honest spirit of our inner child.

Own Your Power

Reclaiming personal power and healing from the aftermath of abuse trauma requires inner transformation. This entails shifting focus from external factors like social status and wealth to cultivating a mindset and behaviors that empower you. Embracing a growth mindset and making conscious choices in each moment propels you toward your goals and helps you regain control of your life, irrespective of circumstances. Reflecting on past experiences where you demonstrated personal power, including making the decision to leave a toxic relationship, reinforces your ability to tap into this inner strength. While external support is valuable, personal power primarily stems from within and is influenced by various factors:

- **Convictions and perspectives:** These are critical elements in the development of personal power. By examining your belief system and finding ideas that may be limiting you, you may replace them with more empowering ones.

- **Internal dialogue:** Your self-talk may either enhance your resolve and conviction in yourself, or it can leave you feeling trapped and miserable. As opposed to seeking approval from others, it matters most to have powerful conversations with yourself, stating the things you need to hear to feel empowered.

- **Talents and capabilities:** Building skills and polishing your abilities boosts your self-confidence and inner power, allowing you to become an expert in areas that correspond with your interests and beliefs.

- **Purpose:** Finding your life's passion or your personal conviction can be another avenue to gaining personal strength. When you discover what actually connects with you, your power and clarity increase. This belief could be transmitted to others, increasing the force of your own authority.

- **Efforts:** It's incredibly important to consistently take purposeful and intentional actions toward achieving your goals and dreams in order to gain momentum and personal power. By breaking down your desired outcomes into manageable steps and taking them one at a time, you are able to create lasting change and regain control over your life (Nichols and Yugay, 2023).

Here are some policies for regaining your personal power:

1. **Develop self-awareness:** Having a clear and accurate understanding of yourself, including your unique characteristics, flaws, thoughts, feelings, beliefs, and motivations, is what self-awareness is all about. This means being aware of your physical, psychological, emotional, and spiritual aspects and how they all interact together. Self-awareness is critical because it allows you to see beyond your human conditioning and enables you to break free from it, ultimately unlocking your full potential.

2. **Accountability:** It all comes down to being able to respond to any event in life from a position of power and authority. This means accepting complete responsibility for your actions and refusing to blame external sources for your predicament. It's an important part of your connection with yourself and a major contributor to personal progress. As spiritual teacher Mahatria explains (as cited in Nichols and Yugay, 2023), it is up to you to

make your life what you want it to be and blaming others or the world at large is not an effective strategy to get there.

3. **Growth mindset:** This is a method of thinking about your talents and intelligence as always evolving. This entails viewing problems as opportunities for progress and accepting failure as a natural part of the learning process. To cultivate a growth mindset, you must first recognize and question any fixed mental assumptions you may have and then prioritize the learning process over outcomes.

4. **Boundaries:** To follow your convictions, you may need to make difficult decisions and be willing to walk the path alone, without depending on the convenience of others or old patterns. As stated throughout this book, this necessitates creating boundaries with people, circumstances, and conduct (including your own) that no longer correspond with your beliefs.

5. **Authenticity:** Embracing and appreciating who you are and working to be the greatest version of yourself while also taking care of your physical, emotional, mental, and spiritual health are all part of this. This involves perseverance and drives to attain the life you want without the approval or affirmation of others. You can create a satisfying and meaningful life for yourself by prioritizing your own well-being.

Your Vision

Even if we believe we are making all the right choices, finding real happiness in life may be a difficult journey. However, exploring and reacting to our spiritual needs may reveal a true road to fulfillment. According to Vishen Lakhiani (2022), life may be split into three parts: experiences, growth, and contribution. With that in mind, consider what you truly want to experience in this lifetime, how you wish to grow and thrive, and what kind of impact you want to have on the world.

Allow these questions to function as a compass, guiding you toward your soul's longings without overanalyzing the replies. Remember that there are no incorrect responses. The goal is to discover the purpose that sparks your spirit and live a really amazing life. Have the courage to aim for the stars and seize any chance that comes your way. Embrace the uncertainty of dreaming big and releasing your unique potential.

Consider a life in which you have infinite financial resources. What kinds of experiences and adventures would bring you joy? Explore areas of love, relationships, sexuality, and social connections. Consider the locations you want to visit, the activities you want to do, and the aspirations you want to make a reality.

Focus on personal growth. What academic interests and talents do you wish to develop? How do you wish to deal with tough situations and learn new languages? Consider what traits you like and desire to have. Consider how you want to present yourself in social situations and create health and fitness objectives. Consider your long and fruitful life, full of joy, purpose, and the capacity to do what you love, even in old age. Consider topics in spirituality that you want to go further into.

Recognize the power of giving back. Contributing to people and the world around us brings us great joy. Consider the different ways in which you can make a difference, no matter how big or small. Think about how you can help your family, friends, society, or perhaps the entire world. Consider the legacy you want to leave and the positive effect you want to make. Volunteering, particular initiatives, or any activity that benefits others and our planet are all possibilities.

By considering these questions and writing down your goals, you are laying the groundwork for a happy life that includes personal development, significant contributions, and endless enjoyment. Embrace the journey of self-discovery and the many possibilities that await you.

Your Goal Statement

Goal statements are essential for personal progress because they provide clarity, direction, and drive. They are brief, strong statements that describe an individual's goals, whether in their personal or professional lives. Setting successful goal statements is critical because it allows people to focus their energy and efforts, match their activities with their ambitions, and track their progress along the way.

Goal statements are valuable because they provide a strong sense of purpose and vision. They serve as guiding beacons, assisting individuals in making decisions, prioritizing activities, and staying on course in the face of daily distractions and problems. Break down your broader dreams into smaller, more achievable steps by identifying precise goals, making progress more feasible, and improving your confidence.

Creating an effective goal statement involves several key steps. First, it's essential to reflect on one's desires, values, and long-term vision. This self-reflection enables individuals to identify what truly matters to them and what they want to achieve. From there, it's important to formulate goals that are specific, measurable, achievable, relevant, and time-bound (SMART). This framework ensures that goals are well-defined and actionable (Butcher and Yugay, 2022).

The creation of a goal statement can be done using a structured process:

1. Start by stating the goal clearly and succinctly.

2. After that, reflect on the significance of achieving this goal and how it fits with your values and aspirations.

3. The next step is to list the precise actions and milestones that must be reached in order to achieve the goal.

4. To add a sense of priority and accountability, it's beneficial to include a timeline or deadline.

It's also essential to examine and revise goal statements on a regular basis. This allows you to stay focused, adjust your techniques as required, and stay motivated on your personal development path. You can retain momentum and continue advancing towards your intended results by measuring progress, celebrating accomplishments, and making necessary modifications.

Goal statements are effective instruments for promoting personal development. They give clarity, direction, and motivation by establishing explicit goals and articulating the procedures required to reach them. Individuals may match their behaviors with their beliefs, stay focused in the face of adversity, and track their progress by developing successful goal statements. These statements need to be reviewed and revised on a regular basis to ensure continued growth and development.

Exercise: The Tree of Life Concept

The Tree of Life exercise is an effective tool for self-discovery and personal development. It enables you to graphically map out the numerous variables that affect your life and learn more about yourself (Weller, 2014). Spend some time doing this exercise by following the steps below:

1. **The Tree:** Begin by sketching a tree. Don't stress about it being flawless; a rough sketch will suffice. This is your representation of the tree of life, complete with a compost heap, roots, ground, trunk, branches, leaves, fruits, flowers, and seeds.

2. **The Compost Heap:** Make a list of any negative influences, past traumas, or limiting ideas that no longer define you. Consider them to be things you want to dismantle and reintegrate as good components of your life.

3. **The Roots:** Write down your origins, such as your hometown, state, nation, or cultural heritage. You might also list notable people or organizations that shaped your childhood.

4. **The Ground:** List the activities and decisions you do on a weekly basis that you have voluntarily selected for yourself. These should reflect your personal passions, interests, and hobbies.

5. **The Trunk:** Make a list of your strengths and ideals. Begin at the bottom of the tree with your values, which reflect your fundamental ideals, and work your way up, listing your abilities and areas of competence.

6. **The Branches:** Write your goals, desires, and aspirations for each branch. These might be personal, community, or universal goals for oneself and the world as a whole.

7. **The Leaves:** Make a list of people who have had a positive influence on your life, such as friends, family, relatives, mentors, or role models. Include everyone who has aided your development and well-being.

8. **The Fruits:** Consider the legacies left to you by the people you named on the leaves. Consider the traits, values, or characteristics you acquired from them. Make a note of these as the fruits of your tree.

9. **The Flowers and Seeds:** Make a list of the legacies you want to leave for others. Consider the positive difference you wish to make in people's lives, whether through compassion, sharing knowledge, or any other meaningful contribution.

10. **Reflection:** After you've finished the tree, try writing about the many components and connections you've discovered. Explore the connections between your roots, values, abilities, and the people in your life. Use this as a safe haven for introspection and deeper understanding.

If you are feeling overwhelmed or anxious that this exercise will elicit powerful emotions or evoke prior trauma, you can instead do it with the help of a therapist, trustworthy friend, or family member. They may provide advice and a listening ear as you travel through this introspective trip.

Take the initial steps toward harnessing the power of your own life narrative. Accept the chance to confront and alter your past so that you can develop and prosper in the present.

By diving deeply into your ambitions and objectives, you've taken a crucial first step toward building a life that genuinely reflects your authentic self. The following chapter will concentrate on transforming ambitions into concrete tasks and methods for accomplishment. You will discover how to narrow down your desires and objectives to those that actually reflect your principles. Prioritizing these objectives will help you channel your energy more effectively during the following two months.

Through practical exercises, reflections, and inspiring techniques, you will be assisted in building a strategic plan. Learn how to make realistic objectives, break them down, and overcome hurdles. Infusing meaning and purpose into your activities can help you achieve your goals.

Chapter 9:

From Dreams to Action—

Strategizing

Your Way to Fulfillment

There is a distinct difference in the process of turning dreams into realities between people who fantasize and talk about big things and those who take brave action to attain them. While dreams might give momentary drive, sustainable transformation needs persistent persistence and self-belief.

Successful people find satisfaction in taking the required steps to make their ambitions a reality. If you struggle with embracing these actions, you can choose to adjust your dream or transform your perspective. You may unlock an infinite drive to attain your goals by appreciating and enjoying the process.

Keep in mind that your dreams are founded in the present. Every step, no matter how tiny, puts you closer to the life you want. Building momentum requires cultivating powerful habits and celebrating accomplishments with fulfillment and purpose.

Believe in yourself and your ability to persevere. Leaving an abusive relationship and going on this path of rehabilitation and rebuilding takes enormous courage. Your ambitions are within grasp. You can make your ambitions a reality with persistence, self-love, and a commitment to enjoying the ride. Keep going because the best is yet to come.

Short-Term and Long-Term Goals

Setting short-term and long-term goals is essential for personal growth and success. Aligning your goals with your core values and aspirations is crucial before starting this journey. Begin by making a comprehensive list of objectives that encompasses all elements of your life, such as your work, relationships, health, personal growth, and so on. This all-encompassing strategy guarantees that you address all critical areas and live a healthy and satisfying life.

To make your goals effective, it is crucial to follow the SMART principle. SMART stands for Specific, Measurable, Achievable, Relevant, and Time-bound. Specificity helps you define your goals, while measurability allows you to monitor your progress. Make sure your goals are reasonable and attainable in light of your existing situation and resources. However, don't be afraid to go just a little beyond what you think is accessible. Align these goals with your long-term vision and ensure they have relevance in your life. Finally, assign a timeline to each objective to create a sense of urgency and accountability.

While long-term goals offer direction and a vision for your future, the key to achieving progress is to break them down into smaller, manageable short-term goals. Short-term goals serve as stepping stones toward your long-term vision, helping you track your progress and stay inspired. You build a clear path to achievement by breaking down your long-term goals into smaller, doable activities. Celebrate each achievement along the road to keep your motivation strong and urge you ahead.

Remember that goal-setting is not a one-time event. Review and reassess your goals on a regular basis, making modifications as circumstances change. Maintain your commitment and be willing to adjust your goals in response to new possibilities and experiences. Embrace the road toward growth and enjoy the process of reaching your goals. You have the capacity to transform your ambitions into actual successes if you have a well-defined master list, SMART objectives, and a methodical way to break them down.

Taking Action

Taking action is the spark for change and the driving factor behind making aspirations come true. It is the pivotal step that drives us ahead, allowing us to realize our dreams and effect substantial change in our lives. Action bridges intention and manifestation by transforming thoughts into tangible results. We build resilience, enhance our capacities, and realize our full potential through action. Taking action, whether it's a modest step or a great leap, is the turning point that sends us on the route to development, accomplishment, and the life we want. So, let us embrace the power of action and set out on the path to living the life we truly desire.

Create an Action Plan

Creating an action plan is an important step toward reaching your objectives and making your dreams a reality. To set yourself up for success, concentrate on a few specific goals at first. Taking on too much too soon might lead to overload and failure. Examine your list of goals and select one to focus on in each aspect of your life. Concentrate your efforts on a short-term objective that seems most meaningful to you or coincides with your long-term vision.

- **Research:** Before taking action, conduct an extensive study on how to attain your desired outcome. Gather information, seek help, and learn from professionals or accessible resources. Having information and techniques at your disposal increases your chances of success and allows you to make more informed decisions along the road.

- **Schedule:** Once your goals and necessary actions have been decided, schedule your action steps. Set aside time for each activity, ensuring that you have adequate time to do them. Be prepared for the unexpected and leave room for flexibility. A well-planned timetable makes you more accountable and assures constant growth.

- **Milestones:** Establish general yearly, quarterly, and monthly milestones to measure your progress and retain focus. Keep these milestones basic and clear so that you can easily monitor your progress. By breaking down your goals into smaller milestones, you can create a roadmap that will guide you to your ultimate vision.

- **Daily routine:** Another essential component of an action plan is the development of a daily routine. Set aside certain hours or blocks of time each day to work on your goals. Integrate these behaviors into your regular routine to make them second nature. Consistency is essential, and a regular routine aids in the maintenance of momentum and discipline.

- **Breaks:** By deliberately planning times for rest and renewal, you can reduce burnout, improve focus, and maintain long-term development. These pauses allow you to recover, reflect, and replenish your energy, allowing you to tackle your responsibilities with newfound energy. Remember that taking prudent breaks is not a sign of weakness but rather a deliberate choice that contributes to your overall success and helps you function at your best.

- **Support:** Recognize that you do not have to accomplish everything by yourself. Allow yourself the liberty to seek assistance and support when necessary. Contact mentors, friends, or support networks for advice, encouragement, and accountability. Collaboration and shared experiences can help you move faster and get useful insights.

- **Intention:** To further solidify your commitment, set a clear intention. Create a sense of accountability by writing or verbalizing your commitment. Consider creating and signing a contract with yourself describing the efforts you promise to execute. Display it openly so that you may see it every day as a reminder of your commitment. Consider making a vision board that illustrates the outcomes you hope to achieve by carrying out the tasks you have committed to (Davis, 2021).

You establish a solid foundation for your path to success by developing a deliberate and detailed action plan. Maintain your focus, adjust as required, and remain committed to the steps that will lead you toward the life you want.

Identify Obstacles

Overcoming obstacles is essential for building an effective action plan. We must identify both external and internal hurdles to our achievement. This involves taking into account the influence of people in our lives who are skeptical or negative. Setting boundaries that align with our goals fosters a supportive atmosphere.

Aside from external factors, situations such as financial limits or a lack of resources might pose difficulties. We must look for alternate answers and accept possibilities for personal development. However, the most difficult impediments are frequently found within us. Our growth is hampered by negative thinking, self-doubt, and fear of failure. Overcoming these obstacles necessitates self-compassion, a development mentality, and requesting help from within and beyond our community.

Recognizing and overcoming these obstacles takes bravery, self-reflection, and endurance. You regain control of your life by aggressively confronting difficulties. Have trust in your resilience, seek assistance when necessary, and keep pushing ahead with conviction. Every difficulty you confront brings out your inner power and provides a chance for personal growth and transformation.

Track Your Progress

Witnessing your progress not only offers you a sense of accomplishment but also keeps you motivated and engaged in the process. After you've established your goals and brainstormed the necessary tasks, it's an effective strategy to keep a physical copy of your action plan. Consider printing your list and displaying it prominently, such as on a bulletin board or at your workspace. As you complete each task, take the satisfying step of crossing them off one by one. This visible recognition of achievement encourages your efforts and enhances your confidence as you grow.

Aside from a paper list, you may use technology to measure your progress more effectively. There is a plethora of task management tools available to help you digitize your action plan. These applications provide features such as reminders and deadlines to assist you in staying on track and properly managing your time. By employing such digital technologies, you can get notifications and alerts that push you to take action or accomplish work before the specified dates. The integration of technology into your action plan improves organization and convenience and encourages effective time management techniques.

You establish a complete tracking system for your action plan by combining the visual gratification of crossing things off on a printed list with the convenience and usefulness of digital technologies. Employ the strategies that work best for you and ensure a clear visual picture of your progress.

Schedule Reviews and Re-evaluations

Creating an action plan is essential for reaching goals, but it's also critical to recognize that plans are not set in stone. Life is unpredictable, and circumstances might change at any time. Successful people recognize that planning entails trial and error, which frequently necessitates revisions. It is critical to evaluate and update your action plan on a regular basis to ensure its relevance and success.

Reevaluating your goals and action plan helps you react to new changes and find more effective solutions. It allows you to reflect on your progress, set priorities, and make required changes. Set frequent checkpoints to assess your progress and see whether your present processes and methods are still serving you or whether new insights can be integrated.

Seek input and counsel from competent individuals with unique points of view. Engaging in candid conversations and receiving advice from mentors, coaches, or support groups can help you refine your approach. Accept adjustments and revisions as natural parts of the process and recognize that they do not reduce your achievement or resolve.

Remember that reassessing and reevaluating your action plan is a sign of adaptability and growth rather than failure. You increase your chances of success by keeping yourself open to change and always upgrading your approach. Accommodate shifts in objectives and approaches while maintaining your overall vision and key principles in mind.

Your action plan is a dynamic tool that may change as you navigate life's uncertainties. Accept the process of trial and error, learn from your mistakes, and look for possibilities for growth and advancement. Regularly evaluating and refining your plan allows you to make educated decisions, stay on track with your goals, and successfully handle unforeseen occurrences.

Celebrate Your Wins

Shifting your focus from the pain of the process to the positive outcomes can bring inspiration. To keep yourself motivated, write down the advantages of reaching your goals. Create a reward system corresponding to your milestones, whether big or small. Celebrate by engaging in self-care, interests, or small pleasures. Material rewards aren't the only way to celebrate your wins; it's also about acknowledging your efforts and accomplishments. Recognize little victories, especially when faced with hurdles or losses. To boost your motivation, share your accomplishments with supportive friends or groups.

Celebrating victories is essential for reconstructing your life, staying positive, increasing self-confidence, and driving determination. Prioritize recognizing and celebrating triumphs because they will bring you closer to your ultimate goals.

Seeing It Through

It's essential to see your goals through to completion if you want to make your aspirations a reality. It is not enough to merely have an action plan; you must also have methods in place to guarantee that it is carried out. A well-thought-out strategy allows you to stay focused, overcome hurdles, and sustain momentum. It gives you a road map to follow, keeping you on course even when confronted with obstacles or diversions. By applying effective techniques and sticking to your strategy, you boost your chances of success and produce a sense of achievement as your efforts bear fruit.

Remember Your Why

Remembering your "why" is critical when pursuing your objectives and staying motivated. It is critical to discern between your genuine ambitions and the expectations of others. You can investigate your intrinsic and extrinsic motivators to determine what you truly desire (Christian, 2020).

Intrinsic motivators stem from within and represent your heartfelt desires. They encompass pursuing behaviors that provide you with true happiness and are consistent with your beliefs, such as personal development, fostering relationships, or pursuing passions. Extrinsic motivators, on the other hand, are motivated by external sources and frequently arise from social or familial pressures. When you think about it, these aspirations may not genuinely connect with your authentic self.

You may determine your genuine motives by asking yourself relevant questions on a regular basis, such as whether your aspirations truly matter to you or if pursuing a goal matches your beliefs. Reminding yourself of your objectives and relating them to your values and purpose can help you stay focused and dedicated to your goals.

It's important to distinguish that both intrinsic and extrinsic objectives may be meaningful as long as you grasp their relevance and avoid chasing hollow goals for the sake of external validation. Consider why you want to pursue a specific goal and the rewards you anticipate. You may guarantee that your efforts are relevant and gratifying by matching your aims with your core values and personal aspirations.

Throughout your journey, revisit your values and purpose to ensure they remain true to who you are. Life circumstances and personal growth may cause alterations in priorities, and it's critical to respect such transitions. Staying connected to your genuine intentions allows you to make necessary modifications to your goals and plans, ensuring that they continue to resonate with your authentic self.

Remembering your "why" ultimately provides you with a compass that steers your choices and keeps you motivated. It gives your path focus, purpose, and a feeling of fulfillment, allowing you to stay dedicated to your goals and handle any hurdles that may emerge.

Visualize Success

Visualizing yourself, taking action, and succeeding is a strong strategy for increasing motivation and driving you to achieve your objectives. When you truly picture your ambitions, they become more tangible and reachable, inspiring you to persevere. Surprisingly, the process of visualizing engages the same brain regions as actually completing the job, resulting in enhanced performance in real-world situations.

When you engage in this practice, close your eyes for a moment and envision the life you want, allowing yourself to get into the details. Write out the specifics of your dreams to gain clarity on what you really want to strive for. The more you practice this visualization, the more you will align yourself with your goals and strengthen your commitment to taking consistent action.

Create an Environment for Success

When taking action toward your objectives, creating conditions for success is critical, and it begins with prioritizing your well-being. It must be acknowledged that feeling perpetually overwhelmed or worn out is neither useful nor sustainable. Taking action should push you beyond your comfort zone while also allowing for ebbs and flows, along with moments of rest and self-care as you develop your abilities and confidence:

- **Let go of perfection:** Set a completion goal instead of striving for perfection and feeling terrible when you fall short. Instead of completing all of your action steps 100% of the time, aim for a more manageable proportion, such as 80%. Recognize that it is normal not to always achieve every objective and that we are only humans (Davis, 2021).

- **Embrace failure:** Allow yourself to fail from time to time. Despite our best intentions, we may struggle to complete some activities. Allowing yourself time to relax and admitting that it's okay to depart from the plan might be useful. Consider giving yourself a limit, such as a specific number of "fails" every day. For example, *I will allow myself six fails every day before declaring the day unproductive.* Use these moments to regroup and get back on track throughout the day.

- **Assess your environments:** Surround yourself with positive, action-oriented individuals, and seek circumstances that encourage you to take action. Spending less time with negative influences and engaging in new connections may be part of this. Taking classes, joining online groups, finding a mentor, or forming a mastermind group may all contribute to a successful atmosphere (Christian, 2020).

- **Control your body's stress reaction:** Cultivate stress-management practices like exercise, meditation, creative outlets, visualization, journaling, restful sleep, time management, and seeking social support. Each person's way of dealing with stress is unique, so try out several strategies to see what works best for you.

By creating an environment that promotes your well-being, cultivates positive influences, and effectively handles stress, you can increase your motivation, stay focused, and take consistent action toward your goals.

Utilize Constructive Outlets for Your Emotions

When taking on a difficult journey, bumps in the road are inevitable and can elicit a variety of emotional responses in us. Suppressing these feelings might be harmful to our physical health and impede our growth. Instead, it is essential to understand and regulate our emotions so that we can make wiser decisions in life.

If we take the time to listen to our emotions, we may be able to use their force to progress in the pursuit of our goals. Rather than allowing negative emotions to consume us, we can redirect them into healthy outlets. Activities such as music and dancing can provide a creative and therapeutic outlet for these feelings. Journaling and meditation, for example, allow us to tune into our emotional condition, gain insight, and find inner peace.

By accepting and leveraging our emotions, we can transform them into powerful instruments for personal growth and inspiration. Rather than being stifled by them, we can embrace them as a source of encouragement and drive, eventually fueling our journey toward achievement.

Prioritize Your Actions Over Their Results

While it is critical to ensure that our activities correspond to our intended results, it is also important not to get excessively focused on the end result. In actuality, it is the journey, the process itself, that is most important. Whether our actions lead to the intended results in three months, a year, or even a decade, we must acknowledge that a significant amount of our lives will be devoted to completing these measures. As a result, it is essential that we gain pleasure and belief from our actions.

Too much attention to the ultimate result might lead to disappointment and frustration if it takes longer to materialize or does not develop exactly as planned. On the other hand, by focusing on the tasks themselves, we might discover fulfillment and meaning in the present moment. When we sincerely enjoy and believe in the actions we take, each activity becomes a worthwhile and gratifying experience, regardless of the end result.

Practice Tenacity

Being tenacious, ferocious, or having grit is all about going beyond skill and harnessing the force of passion and perseverance. It necessitates confronting hurdles head-on and persevering through difficulties. High performers recognize the need for resilience and create mental fortitude to withstand hardship (Duckworth, 2016).

Grit can be developed by anybody since it requires being strong in the face of suffering, fear, or sadness, therefore tapping into our bold and tenacious nature. It entails being precise, detail-oriented, and cautious while being confident, committed, and optimistic. Striving for excellence and persevering in challenging conditions to attain long-term objectives are essential components of tenacity. By embracing these attributes, we may realize our full potential and achieve incredible things.

Work With a Coach

A mentor provides an objective and unbiased viewpoint, supporting you in building successful tactics for initiating and maintaining action. They act as a support system for you during the full process of making your ideas a reality.

The strategic guidance, accountability, and encouragement offered by frequent coaching sessions may be crucial in achieving big objectives and accomplishing transformations. A coach can help you overcome hurdles, stay inspired, and stay focused on your goals. Their knowledge and advice can mean the difference between failure and success.

Exercise: The 1-3-5 Rule

The 1-3-5 rule is a simple and efficient strategy for organizing and prioritizing tasks. It entails breaking down your daily tasks into one major thing, three medium things, and five little things that you need to get done. This rule offers an organized approach to task management and assists you in focusing on the most important and impactful activities.

Take a few minutes at the end of each day to plan your 1-3-5 list for the next day. This way, you can start your day with a clear plan and get right to work. If your job requires regular meetings or unexpected duties, you may need to change the numbers somewhat to account for these requirements.

By reducing your to-do list to 1-3-5 items, you may prioritize your obligations according to their importance and impact. This exercise encourages you to make decisions and ensure that your actions are in line with your goals and priorities. It keeps you from being overwhelmed and keeps you focused on what truly matters.

Remember that time is limited, and you can only accomplish so much in a day. The 1-3-5 rule allows you to take control of your calendar and prioritize things depending on their relevance. This method allows you to be more purposeful with your time and achieve what you have actively selected rather than simply reacting to whatever comes your way.

We've explored the significance of developing a strong and practical action plan to turn your aspirations into reality. You have built the framework for advancement and growth by defining strategies, setting goals, and taking continuous actions toward your aspirations. This process necessitates commitment, resilience, and the capacity to adapt to obstacles that might arise along the road.

As we go on to the next chapter, keep in mind that your journey of self-discovery and personal growth extends beyond the accomplishments and milestones you set out to achieve. The next chapter will help you recognize and embrace your inner wisdom, resilience, and intrinsic worth.

This chapter will stress that real self-esteem and self-love are not obtained entirely from external variables like the accomplishment of tasks or seeking validation from others. It will instead assist you in understanding that self-esteem is rooted in how we view ourselves and absorb our own value. It will provide you with insights and methods to help you create a healthy sense of self-worth, celebrate your progress, and appreciate the unique characteristics that make you who you are.

Chapter 10:

Redefining Yourself—Celebrating Growth and Progress

It's critical to remind yourself that you are knowledgeable, resilient, and worthwhile as you continue on the road of rehabilitation and rebuilding after leaving an abusive relationship. Your healing journey demonstrates your strength and commitment. Remember that self-esteem and self-love are not dependent on external reinforcement or accomplishments; they are based on how you view yourself and internalize your value.

Allow yourself time to consider how your life has altered since leaving the abusive relationship. Remind yourself why you decided to leave and be honest with yourself about the genuine character of the person with whom you were connected. Accept the changes that have occurred and make room for healing. Allow yourself to grieve and consider writing as a way to process your emotions. Forgive yourself, exercise compassion, let go of victimization, and let go of guilt.

Affirmations and gratitude can help you reframe your views. Regain faith in yourself and emphasize self-care. Put yourself first, cultivate mindfulness, and look after your physical health via diet, sleep, and exercise. Allow yourself to feel good and explore the things that make you happy. Celebrate your recovery and progress by concentrating on the journey rather than the destination. Recognize your accomplishments along the journey and consider the fresh prospects that await you. Remember that you deserve a life full of love, respect, and pleasure.

Reflect on How Your Life Has Changed

Reflecting on how your life has evolved since leaving a toxic relationship is a vital part of recovery. Take some time to reflect on why you made the brave choice to leave. Recall your anguish, fear, and emotional turbulence, and reaffirm your determination to make a better life for yourself. It's key to be honest with yourself about who the abusive individual was, admitting their detrimental actions and the terrible influence they had on your well-being.

Recognize and appreciate how far you have come in your healing journey as you reflect. Acknowledge your persistence and courage in breaking free of the cycle of abuse. Recognize the positive developments in your life, such as reclaiming your freedom, restoring connections, or rediscovering your own identity.

Furthermore, while you reflect on your progress, it is critical to identify and address any remaining concerns or worries. It may take some time to fully grasp the degree of your abuse and to process your feelings. Be patient with yourself and seek support from reliable friends, family, or experts who can assist you in navigating these difficult times.

Remember that reflecting on how your life has changed and understanding why you left is a powerful approach that can reinforce your decision, validate your experiences, and continue on the path to healing and rebuilding a happy, loving, and respectful life.

Embrace Your Changes

It's important to recognize that you won't be the same person you were before the abusive relationship, and that's completely okay. Your experiences have shaped you, but they do not define or lessen your amazing qualities.

Recognize and accept that you have come a long way in your healing journey. You have faced challenges, made tough decisions, and taken steps toward reclaiming your life and independence. This shows incredible fortitude and resolve. Appreciate the progress you have made, no matter how small it may seem, and celebrate the inner growth and transformation you have experienced.

Embrace the amazing and strong person you are today. Allow yourself to fully embrace your new identity and the changes you have gone through. As you progress, emphasize self-acceptance, self-love, and self-care. Appreciate your unique qualities, strengths, and abilities that have developed as a result of your perseverance. Surround yourself with supportive and understanding people who recognize your strength and value.

Remember that you have overcome adversity and emerged stronger and more tenacious. Embracing your changes is a powerful act of self-empowerment and a testament to your resilience. You are worthy of love, respect, and happiness, and by accepting yourself as you are now, you open yourself up to a future full of limitless possibilities.

Self-Love

Self-love is a necessary and transformational part of your life's journey. It enables you to show consideration for your well-being, recover from previous pains, and acknowledge your worth. To nurture self-love, it is necessary to engage in various behaviors that encourage self-care and inner healing.

Allow yourself to grieve for the suffering and losses you have endured. Let yourself process your feelings, whether by journaling, conversing with a trusted friend, or getting professional help. By acknowledging the pain you feel, you make room for healing and progress.

Self-forgiveness is an essential component of self-love. Be kind to yourself, giving up the burden of victimization and letting go of blame. Let go of self-criticism and embrace self-compassion. Affirmations and gratitude can help you reframe your views and remind yourself of your true value and the positive aspects of your path in life.

It's also important to learn to trust yourself. Allow yourself to make judgments and decisions that are consistent with your values and instincts. Give yourself some credit. Trust your intuition and respect your own needs and desires.

Additionally, give yourself permission to feel content. Engage in activities that bring you happiness and satisfaction. Explore your interests, hobbies, and passions. Take the time to compliment yourself on a regular basis and believe in the positive affirmations and kind words of others.

Finally, self-love is a lifelong exercise that includes accepting your emotions, forgiving yourself, reframing your beliefs, and believing in your own skills. By fostering self-love, you lay the groundwork for compassion and acceptance, allowing you to live a life full of love, pleasure, and satisfaction.

Self-Care

Making self-care a priority in your life is critical to your overall health and recovery. It entails intentionally attending to your physical, mental, and emotional needs, as well as acknowledging that you deserve to be cared for and nurtured. You may have an improved and more balanced life by emphasizing self-care.

Putting oneself first is an essential component of self-care. This includes setting boundaries, saying no when required, and making decisions that are beneficial to your health. You make room for self-growth and fulfillment by prioritizing your needs.

Mindfulness and being present at the moment are effective tools for self-care. It enables you to tune into your thoughts, feelings, and experiences without being judged. Mindfulness practices such as meditation, deep breathing exercises, or just pausing during the day to halt and breathe can help you feel grounded and find peace and balance in the midst of chaos.

Taking care of your physical health is an important aspect of self-care. This involves feeding your body healthy foods, getting enough sleep, and exercising on a regular basis. Paying attention to your body's demands and providing it with the care it requires will improve not only your general health and energy levels but also your mental health and resilience.

Another important part of self-care is emotional management. Identify and acknowledge your emotions, and then develop appropriate methods to express and regulate them. This might include learning to sit with and process your emotions, doing things that make you happy, getting help from loved ones or experts, or exploring therapeutic techniques like journaling or art therapy.

Self-care breaks should be scheduled throughout the day. Make time to breathe deeply, relax, and rejuvenate. These pauses help you to refocus and recenter yourself, bringing tranquility and renewal.

Self-care is not selfish; it is a critical investment in your own well-being. By prioritizing self-care, you lay a stable foundation for your healing and rebuilding process, allowing you to be your best self in all facets of your life.

Celebrate Your Growth

Celebrating your progress and acknowledging the great strides you have made on your recovery path is a great approach to celebrating your progress. Instead of focusing entirely on achieving a certain objective, shift your attention to appreciating and accepting the transformational process you have undertaken.

Value progress above perfection and be patient with yourself. It takes time to heal and rebuild after leaving an abusive relationship, and it's crucial to remember that growth happens at its own pace. Accept your small victories along this road and appreciate the efforts you've made toward healing and self-improvement.

Take the time to celebrate your accomplishments. Consider the significant moments and accomplishments throughout your journey. It might include identifying moments of personal strength, setting appropriate boundaries, or engaging in self-care routines. Celebrate these achievements as markers of your tenacity, fortitude, and advancement. Allow yourself to feel proud of your accomplishments.

Also, keep in mind that progress is rarely linear. It's normal to experience setbacks or hurdles along the way. Take advantage of these outcomes for learning and growth. Each failure may bring significant insights and strength as you go.

Celebrate your progress by surrounding yourself with individuals who are encouraging and supportive of your efforts. Share your achievements with trusted friends or family members who can offer support and join you in celebrating. Remember that your progress demonstrates your resilience and inner strength.

You may build a sense of empowerment and appreciation for your own improvement by concentrating on the process rather than a single goal, exercising patience, and appreciating your accomplishments. Celebrate yourself as you continue to recover, rebuild, and construct a life that is full of happiness, love, and fulfillment.

Look to the Future

Looking ahead is an exciting part of the journey. It's an opportunity to discover intriguing possibilities, rekindle old passions, and embrace the freedom to live your life as you see fit.

Consider the fresh prospects that await you. Consider the things you once put off or postponed because of the limits of an abusive relationship. Now is the time to revisit your hopes, ambitions, and interests. Start pursuing endeavors that offer you joy and contentment, whether they be hobbies, artistic projects, or moves toward an alternative career path. Welcome the freedom to prioritize your own pleasure and make decisions that reflect your true self.

Furthermore, be open to trying something new. Use this time of rebuilding to get out of your comfort zone and venture into unfamiliar territory. It might be acquiring a new skill, developing a new passion, or participating in activities that challenge and inspire you. Trying something new may broaden your horizons, enhance your self-esteem, and present you with new insights into life.

Remember that the options are limitless as you look to the future. Appreciate the freedom to live a life that reflects your beliefs, interests, and goals. Continue on your road of healing and personal improvement by remaining open to new possibilities and allowing yourself to grow and change.

Accept the rush of excitement and curiosity that comes with exploring new possibilities. Believe in yourself and your ability to navigate the unknown. The future is yours to mold, and with each new encounter, you'll learn more about yourself and your great potential.

This chapter of your life is about accepting that you have all you need to be in charge of your own life. Despite your harsh circumstances, you have always possessed inner strength, perseverance, and beauty. The process of healing and rebuilding after leaving an abusive relationship demonstrates your inner strength and the unshakable essence of your genuine self.

As you reflect on your life, appreciate the changes you've gone through, and enjoy the fruits of your labor, remember that you are a wonderful and wholesome person. Your worth and value have always been part of who you are, and no circumstance can change that.

You have the power to design your future, discover new chances, and follow your ambitions with zeal and purpose. Believe in your own strengths, listen to your inner voice, and believe in your amazing potential.

Be kind to yourself, exercise self-care, and surround yourself with love and support as you continue on this transforming path. Accept the process, enjoy your accomplishments, and be patient with yourself. You are on a road of personal strength, self-discovery, and healing.

Keep in mind that you are knowledgeable, resilient, and useful. You have the ability to design a life that is full of love, pleasure, and fulfillment. Believe in yourself and your potential to succeed. Your future is bright, and you have the potential to achieve greatness.

Conclusion

At the completion of this stage of your long journey, it is important to recognize the incredible venture you have undertaken. You confronted the painful experiences head-on, delving deep into your emotions and trauma with courage and strength. Despite the difficulties and unsettling moments, you deserve a lot of credit for showing up for yourself.

You've learned a lot about trauma bonds in these pages, including how they operate, how to spot them, and how to cope with their profound effects. You've taken the time to enlighten yourself, which has aided your recovery process.

Furthermore, you explored the essential idea of reclaiming your space for healing by establishing healthy boundaries. You've learned to create boundaries with the outside world to protect your well-being, as well as with yourself, to foster self-compassion and self-care.

Financial difficulties, which are sometimes connected with toxic relationships and abuse, may be daunting. You have, however, acquired the tools necessary to overcome the pressure and dread connected with these problems. You've embraced the path to financial freedom, giving yourself the ability to repair and prosper.

You have accepted joy and welcomed light into your life along the way. You have opened the door to a brighter future by engaging in things you enjoy and committing to positive change. You've learned to savor happy moments, allowing them to fuel your progress.

Setbacks were a given as you made your way through this transforming process. Nonetheless, you have learned to recognize and embrace them as a part of your path. By strengthening your resilience, you have equipped yourself to handle the ups and downs of life and have learned to never let them define who you are or derail your progress.

You have even taken the time to reimagine your life, your purpose, and your beliefs. Your vision has become your compass, and you've established a strategy to see it through. You are prepared to follow through on your newfound route with drive and endurance.

Perhaps most importantly, you have made the intention to recognize your own development, progress, and self-worth. Your past scars may remain, but they do not define you. They are evidence of your fortitude and the power you have discovered within yourself.

Throughout this journey, I hope you have discovered the innate beauty, strength, and resilience that you have always possessed. Your past scars may remain, but they do not define you. They are evidence of your fortitude and the power you have discovered within yourself. Your path has revealed your genuine nature, revealing you to be a remarkable person. May your newfound independence inspire you to embrace a revitalized zest for life.

Remember to approach your future with kindness and compassion for yourself but also with ferocity and determination. While it is vital to surround yourself with supportive and encouraging people, it is also important to acknowledge that the power to get your life back on track in a way that brings you happiness lies within you. Whatever life throws at you, you are and always have been a beautiful and worthy person. Today, you shine brighter than ever before, and your radiance is proof of your tremendous growth.

As you move forward, envision an abundant future. Accept the limitless possibilities that await you, knowing that you have the power and resilience to overcome any challenge. You are now prepared to confront life's obstacles with dignity and tenacity, owing to the knowledge and tools you have received.

Finally, remember that you are deserving of a happy, loving, and fulfilling existence. You've emerged from the shadows, reclaiming your power, and rewriting your story. Embrace your newfound liberty, celebrate your growth, and continue to shine your bright light on the world.

Thank you for reading this book. My goal is to nurture hope and resilience and to encourage readers to cultivate a sense of self-advocacy and self-love. As a reader, I value your opinion and feedback. If you could take a moment to leave a brief review at the link below, I would greatly appreciate it.

Also available by Jennifer Alushan

Trauma-Sensitive Parenting: Nurturing Safety, Resilience, and Healthy Bonds Within and Beyond the Home

Purchase today using the QR code below.

References

Acknowledging your trauma. (2022, January 14). The Guest House. https://www.theguesthouseocala.com/acknowledging-your-trauma/

American Trauma Society. (2017, November 23). *10 ways to build resilience.* Trauma Survivors Network. https://www.traumasurvivorsnetwork.org/traumapedias/253

Angela & Daniel. (2022, August 31). *How to love yourself again after a toxic relationship ends.* Alchemy of Love. https://alchemy-of-love.com/expert-relationship-advice/toxic-relationship

Arabi, S. (2017, August 28). *5 powerful healing benefits of being single after abuse.* Psych Central. https://psychcentral.com/blog/recovering-narcissist/2017/08/5-powerful-healing-benefits-of-being-single-after-abuse#6

Are you in a healthy relationship or a trauma bond? (2022, September 8). All Points North. https://apn.com/resources/healthy-relationship-or-trauma-bond/

Batten, S. V. (2022, December 8). *Values clarification for PTSD: Rationale and key concepts.* Psychotherapy Academy. https://psychotherapyacademy.org/act-for-ptsd/values-clarification-for-ptsd-rationale-and-key-concepts/

Being, G. (2022, May 30). *7 stages of trauma bonding.* Grace Being. https://grace-being.com/love-relationships/7-stages-of-trauma-bonding/#stage-1-love-bombing

Bhandari, S. (2022, December 13). *Recovering from trauma.* WebMD. https://www.webmd.com/mental-health/ss/slideshow-emotional-trauma-self-care

Blythe, A. (2018, May 22). *Boundaries with an abusive ex.* Betrayal Trauma Recovery. https://www.btr.org/healthy-boundaries/

Blythe, A. (2020, February 4). *How to get back to yourself after emotional abuse.* Betrayal Trauma Recovery. https://www.btr.org/how-to-get-back-to-yourself-after-emotional-abuse/

Bobby, L. M. (2021a, June 10). *How to repair your self esteem after a breakup.* Growing Self Counseling & Coaching. https://www.growingself.com/how-to-repair-your-self-esteem-after-a-breakup/

Bobby, L. M. (2021b, August 3). *The love, happiness and success podcast with Dr. Lisa Marie Bobby: Repair your self esteem after a breakup or divorce on apple podcasts.* Apple Podcasts. https://podcasts.apple.com/lu/podcast/repair-your-self-esteem-after-a-breakup-or-divorce/id858864457?i=1000392411488

Brickel, R. (2020a, May 15). *How to build resilience as a trauma survivor.* Imago Relationships North America. https://blog.imagorelationshipswork.com/resilience-trauma-survivor

Brickel, R. (2020b, July 9). *How to build resilience as a trauma survivor.* CPTSD Foundation. https://cptsdfoundation.org/2020/07/09/how-to-build-resilience-as-a-trauma-survivor/

Brickel, R. (2021, December 14). *How to set healthy boundaries in relationships after trauma.* CPTSD Foundation. https://cptsdfoundation.org/2021/12/14/how-to-set-healthy-boundaries-in-relationships-after-trauma/

Brickel, R. E. (2020, October 29). *Healthy boundaries in relationships after trauma.* Brickel and Associates LLC. https://brickelandassociates.com/healthy-boundaries-in-relationships-after-trauma/

Brinkley, K. (2019, October 18). *Finding happiness after verbal abuse -- embrace the hurt.* HealthyPlace. https://www.healthyplace.com/blogs/verbalabuseinrelationships/2019/10/finding-happiness-after-verbal-abuse-embrace-the-hurt

Buggy, P. (2017, June 8). *5 steps to define your core values: A compass for navigating life's decisions.* Mindful Ambition. https://mindfulambition.net/values/

Butcher, J., & Butcher, M. (2019, January 16). *Magic happens when you set the right life goals — here's how.* Mindvalley Blog. https://blog.mindvalley.com/life-goals/

Butcher, J., Butcher, M., & Tudor, A. (2023, March 17). *5 ways to crush your personal development goals, according to lifebook creators.* Mindvalley Blog. https://blog.mindvalley.com/crush-personal-development-goals/

Butcher, J., & Yugay, I. (2022, December 23). *How to craft the ideal goal statement to manifest your dreams.* Mindvalley Blog. https://blog.mindvalley.com/goal-statement/

Cadiz, M. (2022, August 1). *Rebuilding finances after financial abuse.* Abuse Refuge Org. https://abuserefuge.org/rebuilding-finances-after-financial-abuse/

Carmody, K. (2019, February 27). *How to start feeling like yourself again after a toxic relationship.* Bolde. https://www.bolde.com/start-feeling-like-yourself-again-toxic-relationship/

Cavoulacos, A. (2020, August 23). *Why you never finish your to-do lists at work (and how to change that).* The Muse. https://www.themuse.com/advice/why-you-never-finish-your-todo-lists-at-work-and-how-to-change-that

Center For Substance Abuse Treatment (U.S). (2014). *Trauma-informed care in behavioral health services.* U.S. Department of Health and Human Services, Substance Abuse and Mental Health Services

Administration, Center for Substance Abuse Treatment. https://www.ncbi.nlm.nih.gov/books/NBK207191/

Christian, L. (2020, October 26). *Taking action: 15 smart ways to go from dreaming to doing*. SoulSalt. https://soulsalt.com/taking-action/

Circle Line Art School. (2014). How to draw A tree: Narrated step by step [Video]. YouTube. https://www.youtube.com/watch?v=ID5H9VVyz4U&ab_channel=CircleLineArtSchool

Cleroux, A. (2014, June 26). *7 things great leaders do to handle setbacks and criticism*. Lifehack. https://www.lifehack.org/articles/productivity/7-things-great-leaders-handle-setbacks-and-criticism.html

Co-parenting with an abusive ex requires setting boundaries. (2022, November 16). Clark Law. https://www.cindyclarklaw.com/blog/2022/11/co-parenting-with-an-abusive-ex-requires-setting-boundaries/

Co-Parenting with an abusive ex-spouse. (2022, February 15). Law Office of Bryan Fagan. https://www.bryanfagan.com/blog/2022/february/co-parenting-with-an-abusive-ex-spouse/

Cooper-Lovett, C. (2018, December 10). *How to reclaim yourself after a toxic relationship*. A New Creation Psychotherapy. https://www.anewcreationpsychotherapy.com/post/how-to-reclaim-your-self-after-a-toxic-relationship

Crawshaw, C. (2018, January 23). *Co-parenting after you've left an abusive relationship*. Today's Parent. https://www.todaysparent.com/family/parenting/co-parenting-after-youve-left-an-abusive-relationship/

Czerny, A. B., Lassiter, P. S., & Lim, J. H. (2018). Post-Abuse boundary renegotiation: Healing and reclaiming self after intimate partner violence. *Journal of Mental Health Counseling, 40*(3), 211–225. ResearchGate. https://doi.org/10.17744/mehc.40.3.03

Davis, T. (2021, March 23). *Taking action: 8 key steps for acting on your dreams.* The Berkeley Well-Being Institute. https://www.berkeleywellbeing.com/taking-action.html

DePaulo, B. (2013). *Are single people mentally stronger?* Psychology Today. https://www.psychologytoday.com/intl/blog/living-single/201305/are-single-people-mentally-stronger

Dexter, G. (2022, January 18). *Healing from relationship trauma.* Verywell Health. https://www.verywellhealth.com/relationship-trauma-5211576#citation-2

Dillmann, S. M. (2011, May 12). *Trauma: True acknowledgement is necessary for healing to begin.* Good Therapy. https://www.goodtherapy.org/blog/scale-traumatic-events/

Divorce in mid-life: Fresh starts, new financial challenges for women. (2018, April 19). Merrill Lynch. https://www.ml.com/articles/divorce-in-mid-life-fresh-starts-new-financial-challenges-for-women.html

Dodgson, L. (2019, May 10). *9 important things to remember to stay strong and love yourself again after a tough break-up.* Business Insider. https://www.businessinsider.com/how-to-love-yourself-again-after-a-break-up-2018-3

Dorko, A. (2015, December 27). *Power of intention: Turn dreams into reality & achieve your dreams.* Without Boxes. https://www.withoutboxes.com/archives/power-of-intention

Draghici, A. (2018, November 27). *Post-Traumatic growth: Can you find happiness after a horrible event?* Happier Human. https://www.happierhuman.com/post-traumatic-growth/

Duckworth, A. (2016). *Grit: The power of passion and perseverance.* New York Scribner.

Edwards, H. (2012, August 23). *Rebuilding your self-esteem after a toxic relationship.* Heather Edwards Mental Health Counseling. https://www.heatheredwardsnyc.com/rebuilding-your-self-esteem-after-a-toxic-relationship/

Emerson, D., & Hopper, E. (2012). *Overcoming trauma through yoga: Reclaiming your body*. North Atlantic Books. https://digitallibrary.punjab.gov.pk/jspui/bitstream/123456789/125422/1/Overcoming%20Trauma%20through%20Yoga_%20Reclaiming%20Your%20Body.pdf (Original work published 2011)

Ferguson, D. (2022, February 28). *Building your dream life starts with defining your values*. Success. https://www.success.com/building-your-dream-life-starts-with-defining-your-values/

Field, B. (2023, April 26). *The dangers of love bombing*. Verywell Mind. https://www.verywellmind.com/what-is-love-bombing-5223611#:~:text=Love%20bombing%20is%20a%20tactic

Finding yourself: A guide to finding your true self. (2015, August 28). PsychAlive. https://www.psychalive.org/finding-yourself/

Five healthy coping skills for facing setbacks. (2023, January 18). BetterHelp. https://www.betterhelp.com/advice/mindfulness/five-healthy-coping-skills-for-facing-setbacks/

Forms of abuse. (n.d.). Womens Law. Retrieved May 3, 2023, from https://www.womenslaw.org/about-abuse/forms-abuse/emotional-andpsychological-abuse

Franklin, F. F. (2016, October 19). *Healing and finding joy after domestic abuse*. Jackson Free Press. https://www.jacksonfreepress.com/news/2016/oct/19/healing-and-finding-joy-after-domestic-abuse/

Fredrek, C. (2018, September 4). *3 stages of recovery from trauma & PTSD in therapy*. Healing Matters. https://healingmatters.ca/3-stages-of-recovery-from-trauma-ptsd-in-therapy/

Gillis, K. (2023, April 17). *Co-Parenting with a toxic ex: 10 tips from a therapist*. Choosing Therapy. https://www.choosingtherapy.com/co-parenting-with-a-toxic-ex/

Girme, Y. U., Overall, N. C., Faingataa, S., & Sibley, C. G. (2015). Happily single. *Social Psychological and Personality Science,* 7(2), 122–130. Sage Journals. https://doi.org/10.1177/1948550615599828

Goldberg, H. (2020, March 22). *To-Do list got you overwhelmed? Simplify things with the 1-3-5 rule.* Shine. https://advice.theshineapp.com/articles/to-do-list-got-you-overwhelmed-simplify-things-with-the-1-3-5-rule/

Goldsmith, B. (2023, March 13). *Recognizing, and exiting, an abusive relationship.* Psychology Today. https://www.psychologytoday.com/intl/blog/emotional-fitness/202303/recognizing-and-exiting-an-abusive-relationship

Greenberg, E. (2019, April 16). *Is couples' therapy useful when one partner is a narcissist?* Psychology Today. https://www.psychologytoday.com/us/blog/understanding-narcissism/201904/is-couples-therapy-useful-when-one-partner-is-narcissist

Griffin, M. (2021, February 2). *Are you putting your values into action? Here's 5 exercises so you can.* LinkedIn. https://www.linkedin.com/pulse/you-putting-your-values-action-heres-5-exercises-so-can-griffin-mbe/

Guerrero, M. (2020, February 12). *Loving yourself after surviving trauma.* Mind Matters MHC. https://www.mindmattersmhc.com/blog/loving-yourself-after-surviving-trauma

Guha, A. (2021, September 20). *How Kate went from estrangement to successful shared custody of her kids.* ABC Everyday. https://www.abc.net.au/everyday/co-parenting-after-a-harmful-relationship/100466444

Gunnell, V. (2016, September 1). *How to turn your dreams into actions.* Medium. https://medium.com/@vaugun/how-to-turn-your-dreams-into-actions-95e78cb44590

Hartney, E. (2022, February 16). *The cycle of sexual abuse and abusive adult relationships*. Verywell Mind. https://www.verywellmind.com/the-cycle-of-sexual-abuse-22460

Hayden, J. (2020, October 27). *Five ways to move on from an abusive relationship*. Aljazeera. https://www.aljazeera.com/features/2020/10/27/five-ways-to-move-on-from-an-abusive-relationship

Ho, L. (2020, May 8). *How to use goals and dreams to achieve personal success*. Lifehack. https://www.lifehack.org/870975/goals-and-dreams

How to deal with financial stress after leaving an abusive relationship. (2022, March 23). Safe in Hunterdon. https://safeinhunterdon.org/how-to-deal-with-financial-stress-after-leaving-an-abusive-relationship/

How to heal after an abusive relationship. (n.d.). My CWA. Retrieved May 3, 2023, from https://www.mycwa.org.uk/how-to-heal

How to heal from emotional abuse in relationships: Therapist approved strategies (2020, September 29). Mind Well NYC. https://mindwellnyc.com/how-to-heal-from-emotional-abuse-in-relationships/

Ishak, R. (2019, March 23). *How to find your confidence after a breakup*. The Everygirl. https://theeverygirl.com/how-to-find-confidence-after-a-breakup/

Johnson, E. B. (2022, May 1). *How to lead a happier life after exiting an abusive relationship*. Practical Growth. https://medium.com/practical-growth/how-to-lead-a-happier-life-after-exiting-an-abusive-relationship-4273fcf35d7

Johnson, J. (2021, October 1). *How to heal after an abusive relationship*. All Points North. https://apn.com/resources/how-to-heal-after-an-abusive-relationship/

Jones, J. (2020, February 25). *Coming home: Reclaiming your space after abuse.* The Downtown Kid. https://thedowntownkid.com/coming-home-reclaiming-your-space-after-abuse/

Jones, J. (2021, February 18). *Getting out: Reclaiming your turf after abuse.* The Downtown Kid. https://thedowntownkid.com/getting-out-reclaiming-your-turf-after-abuse/

Jones, P. M. (2020, June 26). *Turn your dreams into concrete goals.* LinkedIn. https://www.linkedin.com/pulse/turn-your-dreams-concrete-goals-phil-m-jones/

Kaszina, A. (2020, December 2). *How do you set boundaries after abuse?* Recover from Emotional Abuse. https://recoverfromemotionalabuse.com/2020/12/how-do-you-set-boundaries-after-abuse/

Kaszina, A. (2021, August 31). *The loneliness of the emotionally abusive relationship.* Recover from Emotional Abuse. https://recoverfromemotionalabuse.com/2021/08/loneliness-emotionally-abusive-relationship/

Lake, R. (2022, August 26). *How parents' finances impact custody battles.* Investopedia. https://www.investopedia.com/how-parents-finances-impact-custody-battles-5194330

Lakhiani, V., & Yugay, I. (2022a, May 20). *The problem with goal setting and what you can do instead: The 3 most important questions.* Mindvalley Blog. https://blog.mindvalley.com/3miqs/

Lakhiani, V., & Yugay, I. (2022b, December 13). *How to set your true end goals in 3 simple steps.* Mindvalley Blog. https://blog.mindvalley.com/end-goal/

Lambert, C. A. (2022, October 11). *Co-Parenting after divorce when your ex was abusive.* Psychology Today. https://www.psychologytoday.com/us/blog/mind-games/202210/co-parenting-after-divorce-when-your-ex-was-abusive

Lamothe, C., & Raypole, C. (2022, January 11). *What is a toxic relationship? 14 signs and what to do.* Healthline. https://www.healthline.com/health/toxic-relationship#can-it-be-fixed

Lancer, D. (2019, August 3). *How trauma lives on after abuse ends.* Psychology Today. https://www.psychologytoday.com/us/blog/toxic-relationships/201908/how-trauma-lives-after-abuse-ends

Laub, E. (2023, February 23). *The 7 stages of trauma bonding.* Choosing Therapy. https://www.choosingtherapy.com/stages-of-trauma-bonding/

Laura. (2022a, October 3). *Natural ways to calm the nervous system.* Female Worth. https://femaleworth.com/calm-the-nervous-system/

Laura. (2022b, November 5). *How to love yourself after a toxic relationship.* Female Worth. https://femaleworth.com/after-a-toxic-relationship/

Lauren. (2022, January 25). *Boundaries are essential for healing trauma.* LMV Counseling. https://lmvcounseling.com/boundaries-and-trauma/

Leonard, B. (2013, June 18). *What is life purpose?* Taking Charge of Your Health & Wellbeing. https://www.takingcharge.csh.umn.edu/what-life-purpose

Leonard, J. (2021, March 4). *How to let go of the past: Tips for relationships, regret, and trauma.* Medical News Today. https://www.medicalnewstoday.com/articles/how-to-let-go-of-the-past#past-relationships

Lichtman, D. (2021, January 22). *Fear of being alone isn't worth emotional abuse.* Integrated Way. https://www.integratedway.com/fear-of-being-alone/

Lin, F., & Writer's Corps. (2017, December 8). *6 surprising thoughts you might have after a traumatic breakup.* One Love Foundation.

https://www.joinonelove.org/learn/6-surprising-thoughts-you-might-have-after-a-breakup/

Lisa. (2023, March 16). *Finding peace and self-love after an abusive relationship*. NewsBreak Original. https://original.newsbreak.com/@lisa-1602557/2959035675977-finding-peace-and-self-love-after-an-abusive-relationship

Little, K., & Egan, J. (2023, March 17). *Rebuilding your finances after financial abuse*. Bankrate. https://www.bankrate.com/personal-finance/rebuild-finances-after-financial-abuse/

Mandriota , M. (2021, September 8). *7 tips to heal after an abusive relationship*. Psych Central. https://psychcentral.com/health/how-to-heal-after-an-abusive-relationship#takeaway

Maslow's motivational hierarchy. (2023, April 12). APA Dictionary of Psychology. https://dictionary.apa.org/maslows-motivational-hierarchy

Matheson, K., Asokumar, A., & Anisman, H. (2020). Resilience: Safety in the aftermath of traumatic stressor experiences. *Frontiers in Behavioral Neuroscience*, 14. Frontiers. https://doi.org/10.3389/fnbeh.2020.596919

McCulley, P. (2018, September 19). *7 brilliant ways to maintain your self-esteem after a breakup*. Vantage Point Counseling. https://vantagepointdallascounseling.com/relationship-problems/7-brilliant-ways-to-maintain-your-self-esteem-after-a-breakup/

Co-Dependency. (n.d.). Mental Health America. Retrieved May 12, 2023, from https://www.mhanational.org/co-dependency

Meyer, R. (2023, June 2). *Putting your goals into action*. We R Native. https://www.wernative.org/articles/putting-your-goals-into-action

Migala, J. (2020, February 12). *9 signs you're in a healthy relationship*. Everyday Health. https://www.everydayhealth.com/sexual-health/signs-youre-healthy-relationship/

Milstead, K. (2019, June 12). *Setting healthy boundaries after an abusive relationship*. HealthyPlace. https://www.healthyplace.com/blogs/verbalabuseinrelationships/2019/6/setting-healthy-boundaries-after-an-abusive-relationship

Morris, D. (2015, November 5). *Which comes first, vision or values? Does it even matter?* LinkedIn. https://www.linkedin.com/pulse/which-comes-first-vision-values-does-even-matter-deborah-morris/

Murphy, C. (n.d.). *How mothers can support daughters coping with an abusive relationship*. Speak out Loud. Retrieved May 20, 2023, from https://speakoutloud.net/helping-victims-survivors/mothers-concerned-for-daughters-in-abusive-relationships

Nichols, L., & Yugay, I. (2023, March 29). *5 simple strategies to reclaim your personal power*. Mindvalley Blog. https://blog.mindvalley.com/personal-power/

O'Shaughnessy, J. (2019, November 23). *A predisposition to chaos: Setting boundaries after domestic violence*. My Wellbeing. https://mywellbeing.com/modern-therapy-stories/setting-family-boundaries-after-domestic-violence

Oliver, M. (2017, October 3). *5 Ways To Start Setting Boundaries After Emotional Abuse*. Melany Oliver. https://melany-oliver.com/5-ways-to-start-setting-boundaries-after-emotional-abuse/

Owsley, D. (2018, November 26). *Starting over: How to rebuild your finances after escaping a financially abusive relationship*. Relavate. https://www.relavate.org/counseling-help/2018/11/26/starting-over-how-to-rebuild-your-finances-after-escaping-a-financially-abusive-relationship

Pan, M. (2020, August 26). *People remain in toxic relationships because of these reasons*. Medium. https://medium.com/hello-love/people-remain-in-toxic-relationships-because-of-these-reasons-2e2a2d518fa6

Pantazi, J. (2018, October 8). *10 reasons why we stay in toxic relationships.* Youniverse. https://www.youniversetherapy.com/post/10-reasons-why-we-stay-in-toxic-relationships

Perry, E. (2022a, July 27). *The meaning of personal values: How they shape your life.* BetterUp. https://www.betterup.com/blog/meaning-of-personal-values

Perry, E. (2022b, November 23). *How to make an action plan to achieve your goals and follow it.* BetterUp. https://www.betterup.com/blog/how-to-make-an-action-plan-to-achieve-goals

Pollock, A. (2014, February 11). *When it all falls apart: Trauma's impact on intimate relationships.* GoodTherapy. https://www.goodtherapy.org/blog/when-it-all-falls-apart-traumas-impact-on-intimate-relationships-0211145

Potter, B. (2020, June 19). *Coping with the pain of loneliness after a breakup.* Tiny Buddha. https://tinybuddha.com/blog/coping-with-the-pain-of-loneliness-after-a-break-up/

Potts, K. (2020, October 1). *Your goal-getting guide: 6 steps to take action on your dreams.* Life Goals Co. https://lifegoalsmag.com/your-goal-getting-guide-6-steps-to-take-action-on-your-dreams/

Raypole, C. (2020, November 30). *Cycle of abuse: Understanding the 4 parts.* Healthline. https://www.healthline.com/health/relationships/cycle-of-abuse#the-cycle

Raypole, C. (2021, April 29). *How to recognize and heal from relationship PTSD.* Healthline. https://www.healthline.com/health/relationships/relationship-ptsd

Recognizing an abusive relationship. (2017, August 24). American Counselling Association.

https://www.counseling.org/news/aca-blogs/aca-counseling-corner/aca-counseling-corner-blog/2017/08/24/recognizing-an-abusive-relationship

Recognizing the effects of abuse-related trauma. (2018). CAMH. https://www.camh.ca/en/health-info/guides-and-publications/recognizing-the-effects-of-abuse-related-trauma

Resnick, A. (2022a, February 3). *10 ways to heal from trauma.* Verywell Mind. https://www.verywellmind.com/10-ways-to-heal-from-trauma-5206940

Resnick, A. (2022b, November 23). *What is trauma bonding?* Verywell Mind. https://www.verywellmind.com/trauma-bonding-5207136

Ricee, S. (2022, January 11). *Cycle of abuse: An overview and its effects on victims.* Diversity for Social Impact. https://diversity.social/cycle-of-abuse/#9-how-to-recognize-the-cycle-of-abuse-in-relationships-and-take-action

Riordan, H. (2018, April 5). *15 ways to love yourself better after freeing yourself from a toxic relationship.* Thought Catalog. https://thoughtcatalog.com/holly-riordan/2018/04/15-ways-to-love-yourself-better-after-freeing-yourself-from-a-toxic-relationship/

Rivard, K. (2022, July 5). *How I found peace and self-love after a toxic relationship.* Tiny Buddha. https://tinybuddha.com/blog/how-i-found-peace-and-self-love-after-a-toxic-relationship/

Robbins, T. (2019, September 24). *14 proven ways to fall in love with yourself.* Tony Robbins. https://www.tonyrobbins.com/ultimate-relationship-guide/how-to-fall-in-love-with-yourself/

Robinson, L., Smith, M., & Segal, J. (2019, March 21). *Emotional and psychological trauma.* Help Guide. https://www.helpguide.org/articles/ptsd-trauma/coping-with-emotional-and-psychological-trauma.htm

Ross, D. B., & Coambs, E. (2018). The Impact of Psychological Trauma on Finance: Narrative Financial Therapy Considerations in Exploring Complex Trauma and Impaired Financial Decision Making. *Journal of Financial Therapy*, *9*(2), 40–42. https://doi.org/10.4148/1944-9771.1174

Ruffalo, M. L. (2022, February 9). *Self-Blaming depression: Theory and technique.* Psychiatric Times. https://www.psychiatrictimes.com/view/self-blaming-depression-theory-and-technique

Ryu, J. (2023, March 6). *What is trauma bonding? Why you may be misunderstanding this cycle of abuse.* USA Today. https://www.usatoday.com/story/life/health-wellness/2023/03/06/what-trauma-bonding-how-to-break/11365484002/

Saxena, S. (2023, May 18). *How to break a trauma bond: 13 steps from a therapist.* Choosing Therapy. https://www.choosingtherapy.com/how-to-break-a-trauma-bond/

Setting boundaries to create safety: Healing an emotionally abusive relationship. (2020, October 25). Focus on the Family Australia. https://families.org.au/article/setting-boundaries-create-safety-healing-emotionally-abusive-relationship/

7 easy ways to turn your dreams into reality. (2019, January 15). DoSomething. https://www.dosomething.org/us/articles/7-easy-ways-turn-dreams-into-reality

Seven tips for restoring your self-worth after a toxic relationship - mental health training. (2022, July 28). Podcast.Co. https://pod.co/phobia-what-are-you-afraid-of/seven-tips-for-restoring-your-self-worth-after-a-toxic-relationship

Signs of an abusive relationship. (2012, August 9). ReachOut. https://au.reachout.com/articles/signs-of-an-abusive-relationship

Smith, S. G., Fowler , K. A., & Niolon, P. H. (2014). Intimate partner homicide and corollary victims in 16 states: National violent death reporting system, 2003–2009. *American Journal of Public Health*, *104*(3), 461–466. https://doi.org/10.2105/AJPH.2013.301582

Stephens, S. (2018, November 27). *Returning to yourself after an emotionally abusive relationship*. Uplift. https://uplift.love/returning-to-yourself-after-an-emotionally-abusive-relationship/

Stines, S. (2017, January 10). *10 steps to recovering from a toxic trauma bond*. GoodTherapy. https://www.goodtherapy.org/blog/10-steps-to-recovering-from-toxic-trauma-bond-0110175

Stress in america press room. (2022, October). American Psychological Association. https://www.apa.org/news/press/releases/stress

Subramaniam, V. (2015, June 13). *How to rebuild your sense of self-worth after A breakup*. Mind Body Green. https://www.mindbodygreen.com/articles/how-to-find-yourself-after-a-breakup

Survivor Stories. (2019, May 28). *There is a lot of light at the end of the tunnel*. The Survivors Trust. https://www.thesurvivorstrust.org/blog/there-is-a-lot-of-light-at-the-end-of-the-tunnel

Susi. (2018, October 2). *What to do after an abusive partner breaks up with you*. The Hotline. https://www.thehotline.org/resources/what-to-do-after-an-abusive-partner-breaks-up-with-you/

Suskind, D. (2020, December 13). *Rewriting the narrative: 4 ways to reclaim your story after trauma*. Psychology Today. https://www.psychologytoday.com/intl/blog/bully-wise/202012/rewriting-the-narrative-4-ways-reclaim-your-story-after-trauma

Suval , L. (2019, January 18). *The psychology behind remaining in toxic relationships*. Psych Central. https://psychcentral.com/blog/the-psychology-behind-remaining-in-toxic-relationships#3

Taylor, K. (2020, January 7). *Rebuilding your self-esteem after a toxic relationship.* Medium. https://kirstietaylor.medium.com/rebuilding-your-self-esteem-after-a-toxic-relationship-9123d33a3a2b

Tedeschi, R. G. (2020, July 1). *Growth after trauma.* Harvard Business Review. https://hbr.org/2020/07/growth-after-trauma

10 signs of a healthy relationship. (2017, August 28). One Love Foundation. https://www.joinonelove.org/signs-healthy-relationship/

Tewari, A. (2021, June 16). *10 steps to love yourself again after a toxic relationship.* Gratitude - the Life Blog. https://blog.gratefulness.me/how-to-love-yourself/

The Editors. (2023, March 24). *Why do people stay in toxic relationships? (45+ reasons).* UpJourney. https://upjourney.com/why-do-people-stay-in-toxic-relationships

Thurmond, N., & Ekern, J. (2015, February 21). *Healing from trauma and setting boundaries in relationships.* Eating Disorder Hope. https://www.eatingdisorderhope.com/treatment-for-eating-disorders/co-occurring-dual-diagnosis/trauma-ptsd/healing-from-trauma-and-setting-boundaries-in-relationships

Trauma bonding & 10 clear signs to recognize it. (2022, November 8). DiveThru. https://divethru.com/trauma-bonding-10-clear-signs/

Tudor, A. (2023, March 10). *5 tips to set actionable career goals and maximize your potential.* Mindvalley Blog. https://blog.mindvalley.com/career-goals/#h-5-tips-on-how-to-write-career-goals-that-bring-you-closer-to-success

Turner, M. (2023, May 18). *Relationship PTSD: Symptoms & how to heal from PTRS.* Choosing Therapy. https://www.choosingtherapy.com/relationship-ptsd/

Vojta, A. (2022, August 11). *7 expert skills to find peace and self-love after a toxic relationship.* Hello, Love. https://medium.com/hello-love/7-expert-skills-to-find-peace-and-self-love-after-a-toxic-relationship-d164c7ec0374

Waichler, I. (2022, June 9). *Post traumatic growth: Finding meaning after trauma.* Choosing Therapy. https://www.choosingtherapy.com/post-traumatic-growth/

Wallace, S. (2022, July 11). *How to reclaim your identity if you've lost yourself in a relationship.* Remble. https://www.remble.com/post/how-to-reclaim-your-identity-if-youve-lost-yourself-in-a-relationship

Walrack, J. (2023, March 17). *8 personal finance ratios you should be tracking* (Barri Segal, Ed.). US News. https://money.usnews.com/money/personal-finance/family-finance/slideshows/personal-finance-ratios-to-know-at-all-times

Washington, L. P. (2023, April 11). *17 signs of a healthy relationship.* Choosing Therapy. https://www.choosingtherapy.com/healthy-relationship-signs/

Waters, S. (2021, November 19). *How to instill family values that align with your own.* BetterUp. https://www.betterup.com/blog/family-values

Weller, N. B. (2015, February 2). *The tree of life: A simple exercise for reclaiming your identity and direction in life through story.* Nathan B. Weller. https://nathanbweller.com/tree-life-simple-exercise-reclaiming-identity-direction-life-story/

Welsh, E. (2022, November 30). *9 ways to rebuild self-esteem after a toxic relationship.* Seattle Christian Counseling. https://seattlechristiancounseling.com/articles/9-ways-to-rebuild-self-esteem-after-a-toxic-relationship

Wenzel, A. (2020, August 28). *How to break free from the toxic effects of regret.* Brentwood MD. https://brentwoodmd.com/how-to-break-free-from-toxic-regret/

What are your values? (2009, June 21). MindTools. https://www.mindtools.com/a5eygum/what-are-your-values

When emotional trauma shakes your sense of self—how to regain your balance. (2019, April 15). Pathways to Wellness. https://www.pathways2wellness.com/notes-from-p2w/2019/4/15/when-emotional-trauma-shakes-your-sense-of-selfhow-to-regain-your-balance

Woehler, S. (2015, January 7). *10 lessons I learned about grief from ending my 10-year marriage.* Mind Body Green. https://www.mindbodygreen.com/articles/lessons-i-learned-about-grief-from-ending-my-marriage

Wood, K. (2021, July 19). *Five powerful ways to recover from breakup trauma.* Kamini Wood. https://www.kaminiwood.com/five-powerful-ways-to-recover-from-breakup-trauma/

Young, S. (2006, August 25). *Dreams to action.* Scott H Young. https://www.scotthyoung.com/blog/2006/08/25/dreams-to-action/

Zoppi, L. (2020, November 27). *Trauma bonding: Definition, examples, signs, and recovery.* Medical News Today. https://www.medicalnewstoday.com/articles/trauma-bonding#summary

Made in the USA
Las Vegas, NV
29 November 2023